THE SNOWBOARD BOOK

A GUIDE FOR ALL BOARDERS

BY LOWELL HART

W. W. NORTON

New York · London

contents

DEDICATION

In loving memory of Carol Hart, whose courage, strength, spirit, and irrepressible good humor were a source of inspiration to each of her eight children.

First Edition

The text of this book is composed in Fournier with the display set in AG Rounded
Book design by Bill Harvey / Page composition by Christensen Design

Back cover photography (clockwise from top left): Brian Bailey,
Scott Spiker, John Bing, Gordon Wiltsie

Library of Congress Cataloging-in-Publication Data

Hart, Lowell, 1959–
The snowboard book: a guide for all boarders / by Lowell Hart;
photographs by Gordon Wiltsie.
    p.   cm.
Includes bibliographical references.
ISBN 0-393-31692-0 (pbk.)
1. Snowboarding   I. Title.
GV857.S57H37   1997
796.9—dc21   97-30031
                        CIP

W. W. Norton & Company, Inc., 500 Fifth Avenue, New York, N. Y. 10110
http://www.wwnorton.com

W. W. Norton & Company Ltd., 10 Coptic Street, London WC1A 1PU

1 2 3 4 5 6 7 8 9 0

Introduction

Now I know the secret of making
the best persons;
It is to grow in the open air
and to eat and sleep with the earth.
— *Walt Whitman*

Imagine: you and three of your best friends, standing atop a snowy slope. Two feet of untracked powder, deposited overnight, sparkles in the early morning sun. For a moment you stand transfixed, savoring the experience. It seems you can see forever, and you take in the silence, the deep blue sky, and the new-fallen snow highlighting the surrounding peaks.

Then, with exultant whoops, you all explode into action. Courtesies are forgotten as you take off, jockeying with your friends for first tracks. You find your line and delight in the sensation of riding in fresh, deep powder, floating through a series of turns and gently bouncing over undulations in the steep slope. You launch off a small rise, and surprise yourself by sailing farther than you ever have before. The landing is smooth — velvety soft — and you stick it. A friend streaks by, straight-lining it at warp speed, and you follow, then fall into sync behind her as she makes a last series of turns down the final pitch. You stop at the bottom, laughing, and together admire your tracks — a series of perfect figure-eights — and head to the lift for another run. It's the best run you've ever had. And it's on a snowboard.

Whether you are interested in cruising unfathomably deep powder, slicing electrifying arcs into groomed powder, or experiencing the thrill and energy of freestyle, now is the time to find out what all the excitement is about — to learn how to ride a snowboard. Although you may have heard that snowboarding is just "a teen, Generation-X sport," it's actually a great activity for all ages; for people who already enjoy skiing, and for those who don't yet participate in any snow sport.

The first step toward learning to snowboard is as elementary as it is vital: mastery of five key movements. These movements (see page 38) are the building blocks of snowboarding, and the foundation of solid and versatile riding. If you're a first-timer, learning the key movements will allow you to control your speed and direction — *without* painful wipeouts — even during your initial outings on the slopes. Intermediate and expert riders will learn how to apply these movements in order to excel in any snowboarding situation — from effortlessly handling bumps, ice, and challenging snow to carving mind-blowing turns on packed powder, to performing advanced freestyle moves in the terrain park. You'll learn to ride the entire mountain with power, control, and precision, on a great variety of snow conditions and terrain. If you ski, you'll notice that you are able to handle most challenging snow conditions on a snowboard better than on Alpine skis (that's one reason why former skiers rarely look back once they try snowboarding). This is because the equipment is inherently better suited for use in deep or chopped-up powder, wind slab, heavy wet snow, corn snow, or slush.

The Snowboard Book is your complete guide to snowboarding. You'll find comprehensive, up-to-date information on every aspect of the sport, to help you learn quickly and easily. The proven exercises and maneuvers presented are designed to get results *fast*, whether you're a beginner or an experienced rider. The product of more than a decade of daily on-snow research, this book probes such important questions as what, exactly, are the performance characteristics of a snowboard in ultra-deep powder,

in the air, or carving turns at high speeds (tough work, but somebody had to do it!). It also is the result of countless hours spent exchanging information with students and other snowboard and ski teaching professionals: people who live their passion — and enjoy sharing it with others. It was written along creeks rushing fresh with snowmelt, in sweet-smelling spruce groves, and on sun-warmed boulders. Inspiration came on early-morning hikes to out-of-the-way powder stashes, while cruising corduroy at mid-day, and during late-afternoon halfpipe sessions. This book came together, for the most part, outside, in the mountains. I humbly hope it is as much fun to read as it was to write.

Although the information presented will help all snowboarders, you will not get the results you desire without taking snowboarding lessons. Professional instruction will enhance the content of this book and make snowboarding easier to learn and more fun at any level. And in snowboarding, the better you get, the better it gets!

Snowboarding is still a young and rapidly changing sport. As equipment design continues to evolve and new construction materials are employed, technique also will evolve. In this sense, snowboarding is, and always will be, a work in progress, and, with time, will become an even more fun and exciting sport.

I can hardly wait!

— *Lowell Hart*

TheEvolution ofaRevolution

boards: where they came from and where they're going

1

boards: where they came from and where they're going

snow, rather than wallowing through it. The discovery of ancient skis preserved in Scandinavian and Finnish bogs and petroglyphs depicting people skiing suggest that skis were developed well over 5,000 years ago.

The snowboard developed not as a result of a need to go places, but as a result of another human need: to have fun. During the mid- to late 1960s, the music of the Beach Boys and Jan and Dean and films such as Bruce Brown's *Endless Summer* popularized the surfing lifestyle. Not surprisingly, during the same period, surfers and skateboarders were trying to bring their summertime stoke to snowy winter hills. As early as 1963, Tom Sims (snowboard pioneer and founder of Sims snowboards) is said to have built and used prototype skiboards inspired by skateboards.

DEVELOPMENT OF THE SNURFER

Snowboarding lore has it that on Christmas Day, 1965, Sherm Poppen was looking for a way to amuse his rowdy children. In his garage he nailed a platform on top of two skis and created the first prototype snurfer. Poppen worked with the Brunswick Corporation (makers of boating, billiard, and bowling equipment). He was convinced that

Skiing evolved from a basic human need: to go places. In wintry climates, where deep snow made walking even for short distances next to impossible, skis were an easy, reliable way to hunt and travel. The long surface of the ski would keep a person on top of the

the wood lamination process used to produce bowling alley gutters could be adapted to create an improved snow-surfer, and soon thereafter Brunswick turned out the first snurfers.

Snurfing technique was elementary — you pointed the thing downhill and hung on. You could make turns on snurfers, but only in soft snow. They were used exclusively on backyard hills and snow-covered golf courses. More often than not, a run on a snurfer would end in a spectacular crash.

The world's first snurfer contest was held on February 18, 1968 at Blockhouse Hill in Muskegon, Michigan. Subsequent races (held annually until the late 1970s) attracted riders from all over the country, including people who would become snowboarding pioneers. These competitions spawned equipment modifications and improvements.

In 1979, a surfer from Long Island showed up with a custom board equipped with over-sized rubber bands to secure his feet to the deck. Jake Burton Carpenter (founder of Burton Snowboards and a seminal figure in

NATIONAL SNURFER CHAMPIONSHIPS (Above right) 1978 at Blockhouse State Park, Muskegon, Michigan: Snurfer at the starting gate on a SuperPro racing model (third-generation board). **(Above left)** Snurf racing technique was primitive: you pointed the board downhill and hung on.

THE SNURFER vs. THE SNOWBOARD

State-of-the-art snurfers featured a "power cord," V-shaped base, and grip tracks for better traction. Snurfers came in two models – standard and competition – and sold for less than $30. Sales of snurfers numbered in the hundreds of thousands. Snowboards are available in scores of models, they sell for hundreds of dollars each, and worldwide sales number in the millions.

SNURFER Sherm Poppen invented the snurfer by nailing two old skis together for his kids to play on. It was so much fun he went on to produce snurfers. The most commercially successful of the protoboards, the snurfer first appeared in 1966. Hundreds of thousands of snurfers were sold in the late 1960s.

the development of the sport) was not allowed to compete on his modified board in the snurfer race. However, a special "open" category was added, which Jake easily won. Later competitions, such as the National Snowboarding Championships (first held at Suicide Six, Vermont, in 1982), and the World Championships (held the following year at Soda Springs, in California), continued to provide events that allowed board designers to exchange ideas and test their latest modifications.

EVOLUTION OF EQUIPMENT

Riding up lifts and boarding down trails at ski areas probably wasn't on the minds of snowboard pioneers — at least at first. In fact, the earliest snowboards were built to be used in the backcountry. But even in the backcountry, all is not deep powder, so boards that could perform on ice and hard snow as well as in powder were developed, utilizing Alpine ski design and technology to enhance performance. Thus, through the mid- and late 1980s, snowboards were built more like Alpine skis than like surf- or skateboards.

SKI AREA ACCEPTANCE

Through the protoboard years, most ski areas did not allow snowboarding on their slopes.

PRIMITIVE SNOWBOARD HUMOR

As snowboarding was introduced to ski slopes in the mid-1980s, there were challenges to the harmonious integration of the two sports, often caused by the riders themselves. The attitude and lifestyle of most snowboarders struck fear in the hearts of more conservative skiers, who often confused pubescent rebelliousness with a legitimate sport. Here are a few surviving snowboard jokes from that period:

Q: "How does a snowboarder introduce himself?"
A: "Whoa! Sorry, dude!"

Q: "What does a snowboarder use for birth control?"
A: "His personality."

Q: "Why do snowboarders smell?"
A: "So blind people can hate 'em too."

Q: "What do you call a snowboarder without a girl-friend?"
A: "Homeless."

Q: "What's the difference between municipal bonds and snowboarders?"
A: "Municipal bonds eventually mature and generate income."

Q: "How do snowboarder brain cells die?"
A: "Alone."

Early equipment did not yet work very well on hard packed slopes, and area managers were understandably concerned about safety. They didn't want anyone on their slopes to be put at risk by the newfangled boards. As a result, many ski areas allowed people to snowboard only after they passed a certification course to ensure that they could ride safely. As the design of snowboards, boots, and bindings evolved to allow efficient riding on hard snow surfaces (and as growing numbers of riders petitioned ski-area operators to let them use the lifts), forward-thinking areas began to allow snowboarders on their slopes.

At these resorts, professional instruction ensured that riders learned to snowboard safely. The first snowboard instructor's manual, published in 1987 by the Professional Ski Instructors of America (PSIA), established effective, standardized methods for teaching people how to ride. As riders became more proficient — and visible — at ski areas, interest in the sport quickly grew. Areas started to recognize that snowboarders represented a sizable new market, and began to design programs, facilities, and events to attract snowboarders.

EARLY BURTON BOARDS The earliest snowboards incorporated surfboard design features such as swallowtails and fins. As competition and the quest for higher levels of performance through a wide variety of snow conditions and terrain drove equipment modifications, snowboard manufacturers borrowed from Alpine ski technology. Plastic bases, metal edges, sidecut, and camber are all ski design features that were adapted for use on snowboards.

INTEGRATION ISSUES

Even though snowboarding was allowed at ski areas, obstacles to acceptance arose during the first few years of this new activity. Most riders were young, boisterous, and exuberant to the point of recklessness. Snowboarding's in-your-face image inspired some riders to be openly antagonistic toward

GOOD-BYE TWIST AND SHOUT

Snowboard bindings are not designed to release in a fall because snowboarding does not allow independent twisting of the lower legs. Not surprisingly, studies show that there are far fewer damaging injuries to knees among boarders than among Alpine skiers. Rejoice!

ELAN SCX ALPINE SKIS AND BURTON CARVING BOARD Through the years, snowboard manufacturers incorporated concepts and materials from Alpine ski design, such as camber and sidecut, plastic bases, and metal edges, to enhance performance. Recently the roles have reversed. Inspired by the magnificent arcs that skilled riders are able to scribe down a slope, Alpine ski manufacturers have introduced "shaped skis," which feature the same pronounced sidecuts as carving snowboards. On board or skis, big sidecut equals big fun.

people on skis; and the media, always eager for sensational stories, hyped a so-called "war" between boarders and skiers. Snowboarders were blamed for everything from birth defects to global warming. Some ski areas promoted themselves as places where boarding was banned — sanctuaries against the evil scourge spreading over the slopes. However, as snowboarding's popularity has increased and the sport has become more mainstream, most misconceptions have fallen by the wayside.

SNOWBOARDING UNBANNED

In 1985, only 7 percent of U.S. ski areas allowed snowboarding. Today more than 97 percent of them do, and more than half have halfpipes. If you're planning a winter vacation and you or someone you are traveling with wants to snowboard, don't go to the following areas. As of the 1996–97 season they are the only ones that still do not allow snowboarding:

Alta, Utah
Appalachian Ski Mountain, North Carolina
Aspen Mountain, Colorado
Blue Mountain, Pennsylvania
Cascade Mountain, Wisconsin
Deer Valley, Utah
Fiesta Snow Play, New Mexico
Granlibakken at Lake Tahoe, California
Mad River Glen, Vermont
Nordic Mountain, Wisconsin
Perfect North Slopes, Indiana
Sapphire Valley, North Carolina
Sundance, Utah
Taos, New Mexico

BOARDER PATROL In an effort to integrate snowboarders (who were still new to the slopes) with skiers, many resorts encouraged patrollers to get "on board." Patrollers who choose to ride boards must pass the same exacting tests — such as pulling a heavily loaded toboggan through the bumps — as patrollers on skis.

WORLDWIDE GROWTH

Today, snowboarding is one of the fastest growing sports, enjoyed by millions of people worldwide. It is no longer solely the province of rebellious, image-conscious adolescents. In fact, the segments of the snowboarding population that are expanding the most rapidly are adults, small children, and women. And, in an ironic switch, snowboarding now influences Alpine ski design. Inspired by the electrifying arcs that skilled riders on big sidecut snowboards are able to scribe down a slope, ski manufacturers now make skis shaped like snowboards, that feature pronounced sidecuts and shorter lengths.

In little more than two decades, snowboarding has grown from its humble snurfer roots to become an official Olympic sport; men's and women's events include giant slalom races and freestyle competition in the halfpipe — further evidence that the sport of snowboarding has been accepted worldwide.

Text continued on page 16

MO' FUN = MO' OFTEN

Most boarders love their sport so dearly that, on average, a boarder is on the slopes three times more often per year than a skier.

SNOWBOARD SLALOM New sports instantly come of age when they are ushered into Olympic competition. Snowboarding made its Olympic debut with giant slalom and halfpipe events, but new events, like boardercross, will soon follow.

Snowboard Competitions

Snowboarding competitions have been around almost as long as people have been riding, whether on snurfers or protosnowboards. Not surprisingly, equipment and technique have evolved largely through competition. At each contest, board designers test their latest ideas against the best riders and equipment. As the sport has evolved, so have snowboarding events. The earliest snurfing contests were straight-down-the-hill events that tested speed (and balance: Often the winner was the contestant still standing on his snurfer across the finish line). As boards became more controllable, snowboard events began to mirror ski events, such as the slalom and giant slalom, in which competitors negotiated turns through a course. Shortly thereafter, freestyle skateboarding's influence was felt as snowboarders began to compete in the halfpipe.

Today the limits of snowboarding continue to be pushed. In addition to the Olympic events (giant slalom and halfpipe), the world's best riders are discovering what's possible on a board in new and exciting events such as boardercross, big air, radical carving, and extreme contests. If you enjoy a competitive challenge, some of the most rewarding experiences you can have on a board will occur in competition. And there are organized events for a wide range of ages and abilities, from local amateur fun races to highly competitive national events. Here are some of the events in which you can participate. **Timed events** (slalom, giant slalom, downhill) The challenge here is to pilot your board through a set

BOARDERCROSS Inspired by motocross, the object is to beat five other competitors sharing the hill with you.

GIANT SLALOM For the more traditional, snowboarding also offers slalom and giant slalom.

course in the fastest time. Slalom courses require quick, tight turns. Giant slalom and downhill events feature, respectively, longer turns and higher speeds. Timed events demand precision and speed. Most ski areas set aside a recreational racing practice course (usually an easy giant slalom course). For a nominal fee you can practice so you'll be ready on race day.

Judged freestyle events (halfpipe, slopestyle, big air) Competitors are evaluated by a panel of judges as they perform freestyle tricks. Performances are judged according to amplitude, execution, difficulty of maneuver, and overall impression. Halfpipe events occur in the halfpipe, slopestyle events in the terrain park, and big air off of a big jump.

Boardercross The object is to quickly navigate down a challengeing obstacle course featuring big jumps and sharp corners. The distinguishing feature is that you share the course with five other riders, each one determined to beat you down. The action is fast and furious in this motocross-inspired event. The fastest two riders out of any heat advance to the next heat, with the overall winner being the fastest one in the final heat.

Radical carve Athletes on snowboards and super-sidecut skis compete head-to-head on a water-ski-inspired course. Competitors race through a course of "buoys" configured in sets of three. Racers may turn around any buoy in a set, but are awarded bonus points for turning around the farthest buoys in a set.

Powder eight Pairs of competitors try to make the best series of figure-eight turns on an untracked powder slope. Contestants are judged on synchronization, rhythm, symmetry, and roundness of turns. Enter a powder-eight contest if you can. At the very least you are guaranteed fresh powder.

Extreme These contests combine elements of backcountry and mountaineering. Competitors ride steep, exposed lines that are just shy of suicidal. Judges, equipped with telescopes, evaluate the proceedings from the comfort and safety of the base of the mountain. Participants are judged on technical difficulty, line, speed, and air. Not for the faint of heart, extreme competitions attract the nation's best backcountry riders.

Text continued from page 13

INTO THE FUTURE

In the future, all areas will allow snowboarding, with the most successful ones catering to the needs and wishes of snowboarders: Benches will be provided at the top of lifts for boarders to sit on while fastening their bindings; trail layout will be free of long, flat runouts; and exciting terrain parks will provide freestylers with safe areas in which to perform their aerial acrobatics. Snowboarding will continue to grow, and will attract new markets and age groups.

Equipment — and technique — will continue to evolve. Space-age materials and construction techniques will create boards that are lighter and more durable. Boots and bindings will be easier to get into and out of, and will allow for better transmission of energy to the board.

Snowboarding will be even easier to learn, and riders will continue to push the limits. Freestylers will launch bigger air and perform more complex tricks. Racers will ride at higher speeds. Backcountry riders will put up more extreme lines, combining technical mountaineering skills with snowboarding. The distinctions between the different facets of the sport will further blur, with extreme riders throwing freestyle flips off backcountry cliffs, racers competing in timed courses that include judged freestyle jumps, and so on. Even Mount Everest may one day be snowboarded from its snowy summit — maybe by you!

all about boards:
from tip to tail and
from freestyle to freeriding

2

all about boards:
from tip to tail and
from freestyle to freeriding

unprecedented lightness and durability. Each piece is precision engineered for a specific type of riding; and boards, boots, and bindings all deliver levels of performance undreamed of by even the most visionary early snow-boarders.

In addition to the all-mountain, or freeriding, boards that do many things fairly well, there are performance boards designed for particular styles of riding. Whether you're into freeriding, freestyle, or high-performance carving, there's a board, boots, and bindings designed to give you the ultimate ride. Of course, with such specialization come trade-offs: Similar to a baseball player wearing a catcher's mitt at shortstop or a cyclist riding a mountain bike in the Tour de France, using a specialized snowboard for its specific purpose allows you to achieve the highest possible performance in that area, but performance is sacrificed in other areas. Knowing what you want to do on a board — whether it be busting outrageous freestyle moves, carving electrifying arcs, floating through deep powder, or simply enjoying elegant cruises — will enable you to make the right decisions when buying equipment.

Today's equipment has come a long way from the protoboards of the 1960s. Boards, boots, and bindings have evolved and enable riders to learn and progress at an astonishingly rapid rate. Aerospace composites are often used as construction materials, giving equipment

SNOWBOARD ANATOMY
What You See

TIP AND TAIL are the two ends of your board. The tip is upturned to help the board glide

THREE BASIC SETUPS

Stomp pad

Soft boot

Two-strap binding

Freestyle

Leash

Soft boot

Three-strap binding

Stomp pad

Leash

Freeriding

Hard boot

Hard boot or plate binding

Carving

CAP CONSTRUCTION
(top) generally produces
a board that rebounds
quickly when flexed.

SANDWICH CONSTRUCTION
(bottom) generally
produces a strong sidewall
that provides excellent
carving performance at
high speeds.

over the snow. The tail of freestyle and many freeriding boards is greatly upturned so it can be ridden backward as well as forward, called fakie or switch riding (see page 110). The tail of an Alpine carving board is upturned, but barely so. This provides more edge contact and running surface for the board. The slight upturn on the tail also aids in releasing the board from a turn, but is not best for fakie riding.

THE BASE is the polyethylene surface on the bottom of your board. Two types of polyethylene are used: extruded and sintered. Extruded bases are inexpensive and easy to repair. Sintered bases hold wax best, are very durable, and glide faster than extruded bases. They also cost more and are more expensive to repair.

BINDINGS fasten the board to your boots. They are designed to work with either soft boots (used primarily on freeriding and freestyle boards) or hard boots (used primarily on carving boards).

THE SAFETY LEASH keeps your board with you, and is required at most ski areas.

THE TOPSHEET AND SIDEWALLS cover and protect the internal components of your board. On "cap" snowboards, the topsheet stretches clear to the steel edges, and serves as the sidewall as well.

EDGES are the $1/16$-inch steel strips running along the perimeter of the base. Sharp edges allow your board to grip the snow, giving you control.

INSERTS are the holes that hold your binding screws. A few boards do not have inserts: you screw your bindings directly onto mounting plates built into the board.

CAMBER is the arch that's built into your board. To see it, lay your board flat on a hard floor. Camber helps distribute your weight more evenly to the tip and the tail of the board, making the board both easier to turn and more stable at speed and on hard snow.

SIDECUT makes your board turn. Viewed from above, notice that the tip and tail are wider than the middle, where the sidecut creates an hourglass shape. When you tilt your board up on its edge and bend it so that the entire edge stays in contact with the snow (your board bends this way through a turn), you can see that the sidecut describes an arc. The board's hourglass shape will always turn it in the direction in which you tilted it.

BOARD FITTING

To make learning easier – or to achieve higher levels of performance – your board must fit you well. Generally, a board fits if (when placed on its tail) it reaches somewhere between your upper chest and nose, though bear in mind that certain riding situations may demand longer or shorter boards. Freestylers, who specialize in spin tricks, typically choose shorter boards while racers, who compete in speed events such as super-G or downhill, use longer boards.

THE STOMP PAD is located between the bindings. It provides traction for your rear foot when skating across flats and approaching lifts with only your front foot in the binding. Not all boards have stomp pads, but I encourage beginners to buy boards with them or ask their dealer to install one.

What You Don't See

When you look at your snowboard you *don't* see the years of research and development and hours of product testing (or should I say playing?) that went into making your board — but it's there. You also don't see your board's internal components. But rest assured that the guts — the core material, fiberglass wrap, adhesives, and internal dampeners — work together to give you a board that is light, durable, and able to deliver the highest levels of performance and fun.

FLEX PATTERN refers to how and where the board bends. Today's technology allows boards to be soft flexing tip to tail, but stiff torsionally. Imagine drawing a straight line down the center of your board from tip to tail. The amount of twisting that the board will allow along that axis is its torsional flex. Less torsional flex allows a board to grip ice and hard snow; more torsional flex makes a board more "forgiving," but less responsive.

CORE MATERIAL is the substance around which the structural fiber layers are wrapped. Usually made of wood or foam, a board's core needs to be light, resilient, and durable.

INTERNAL DAMPENERS absorb vibration. Made of thin, dense rubber or other compounds, they are strategically located in the board to reduce vibration and chatter without making the board feel mushy or lifeless.

FIBERGLASS WRAP is the major structural component of a snowboard. Different weaves and placements of fiberglass within a board can influence its flex pattern, and its strength and weight.

ADHESIVES glues and epoxies hold the board's components together. Light weight and durability are key considerations.

METAL MOUNTING PLATES are sometimes

KIDS' BOARDS

As snowboarding grows in popularity, younger children are learning to ride (some ambitious parents start their kids as young as 2½ years old). Here are a few important considerations when shopping for a board for your child:

● The board should be narrower than an adult model. Any width greater than the length of a youngster's foot will make edging movements – and control – exceedingly difficult.

● Select a soft-flexing board so that a child's lighter weight can bend it.

● The board should be the right length for ease of control: Set the board on its tail and hold your child up against it – if the tip reaches somewhere between his chest and chin, the board is a good fit.

used to anchor the binding screws. Because this limits the adjustability of stance angle and width, most manufacturers use inserts instead.

SNOWBOARD STYLES

Snowboards come in a surprising variety of shapes and sizes. Although all boards can get you down the mountain, using a board that matches the type of riding you enjoy the most will give you the best performance and the greatest amount of fun from your ride.

Freestyle Boards

These boards are made for performing freestyle tricks: spins, airs, and fakie riding. Generally short, light, and soft (flexible), this is the board of choice if you're planning to spend most of your time in the halfpipe or terrain park. A freestyle board that is perfectly symmetrical along its length and width, with equal distance between the bindings and the tip and tail, is called a *twin tip*. One with a distinct tip and tail, and with the bindings mounted slightly aft of center is a *directional board*. Wider and softer than freeriding or Alpine carving boards, freestyle boards are good all-mountain boards, especially in soft powder, where they float well and flow through the bumps. Freestyle boards are an excellent choice for a beginner; their soft flex makes them forgiving and easier to turn. Designed with less sidecut and camber than other styles, they don't hold a carved turn at speed very well, however. Freestyle boards are paired with soft boots and bindings (see page 19).

Freeriding or All-Mountain Boards

Freeriding snowboards bridge the gap between freestyle and Alpine carving boards. They are all-mountain, go-anywhere, do-anything boards. They do many things well, but aren't able to perform at the highest levels for either freestyle or Alpine riding. You won't see the winner of the Olympic giant slalom using a freeriding board, for example. Freeriding boards are typically turned up at both ends, which lets you ride fakie, float well in powder, and perform freestyle maneuvers easily. They are fairly soft flexing (though stiffer than a freestyle model), providing room for error, and thus making them excellent beginner boards. Yet freeriding boards have a fair amount of sidecut and camber, allowing you to carve precise turns. Either soft-boot or hard-boot bindings can be used with these boards.

Alpine Carving Boards

Alpine carving boards are designed to make exciting, high-speed carved turns. In look and ride they are similar to high-performance "super-sidecut" Alpine skis. On carving

THE LIMITS OF NARROWNESS

In competition, the limit on board narrowness has been set at 14 cm waist width for boards over 129 cm long. Although narrower boards can perform exceptionally, allowing competitors to make lightning-fast edge changes and get closer to gates than with wider boards, they have been determined by race officials *not* to be snowboards, and are banned on the circuit. If you can find a narrower board, try it . . . if it's banned, it *must* be good!

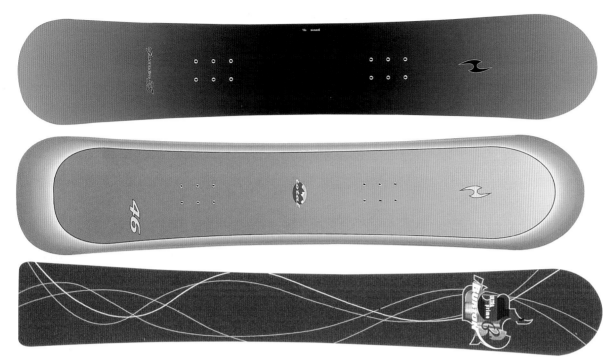

FREESTYLE BOARD Generally shorter and softer flexing than other types of boards, freestyle boards are great for tricks, spins, aerials, and riding fakie. They are also good boards for beginners.

FREERIDING BOARD Freeriding boards combine elements of both freestyle and carving boards. Like freestyle boards, they are turned up at both ends, allowing you to ride fakie as well as forward, and to perform exciting tricks. However, they are stiffer and longer than freestyle boards, making them more stable at speed and able to ride through a greater variety of snow conditions.

CARVING BOARD Typically stiffer and narrower than other boards, carving boards are capable of blasting arcs at high speeds and making lightning-fast edge changes. Although they can be ridden fakie, they perform best when ridden forward.

BUYING A USED BOARD

Here's a checklist to run through before you buy a used board.

Overall condition Does it look damaged or abused? Do stickers or duct tape cover holes, cracks, or dings?

Edges They should be rust free, straight, and smooth. If the edges are thin, it means they have been filed a lot, and may not have many tunes left in them.

Base It should be free from large scrapes or gouges.

Sidewalls No cracks. No holes. If not severely damaged, edges, base, and sidewalls can be repaired by a skilled technician.

Camber Lay the board on a flat, hard surface and check underneath its center: There should be an arch of at least ¼ inch between the base of the board and the surface underneath it. No camber equals a lifeless, unresponsive board.

Check for true With your board on a flat surface, try rocking it gently side to side. Both edges should contact the surface near the tip and tail, so the board should not rock. If it does, it is bent and will not ride well.

SOFT BOOTS Light and easy to get around in, soft boots are the most popular boots sold in the United States today. They feature a lace-up outer boot surrounding a soft, supportive inner boot. They allow for a wide range of ankle motion (useful in freestyle applications) and also work well in powder and for beginners.

HARD BOOTS Hard-shell boots are becoming increasingly popular, particularly as more skiers get into snowboarding. Plastic boots provide the leverage necessary to make powerful edging movements at high speed. That's why they're used by carvers and racers. They're also useful in chopped-up snow, on ice, and in the bumps.

boards, only the tips are upturned. Although you can ride them fakie, they perform best going forward. Often used for racing and sometimes called "race" boards, they are narrower than freestyle or freeriding boards, enabling quicker edge changes and better edge holding power at speed. Expert skiers who take up snowboarding generally appreciate the performance of carving boards, although their stiffness makes them more difficult to use for beginners. Carving boards are typically paired with stiff, plastic-shelled boots and plate bindings, or, less frequently, with a three-strap soft-boot binding.

BOOTS

Snowboard boots, soft or hard, are carefully designed for riding. Do not use any other type of

footwear, such as Sorel-style pac boots, snow sneakers, or mukluks, for snowboarding. Snowboard boots (together with bindings) have built-in support that helps to efficiently transmit the energy created by your movements to your board. The soles are shorter than on other similarly sized footwear in order to diminish the possibility of toe and heel overhang. As with boards, most boots are designed for specific riding styles and are matched to the appropriate board and binding.

Soft Boots

In appearance, the canvas, leather, and rubber exterior of a soft snowboard boot looks like a pac boot or a pregnant, high-top basketball sneaker. But the resemblance stops there. Unlike a pac boot or sneaker, a snowboard boot provides you with internal support that helps you to easily control your board. Soft boots allow a fairly wide range of ankle motion, which makes them preferable for freestyle boarding and for soft snow conditions. They're great for beginners because they are soft and allow more room for error. They are warm, comfortable, and easy to walk around in — you can even drive a

BOOTS FOR WOMEN

Most manufacturers have expanded their lines to include boots designed to fit a woman's foot and lower leg. A woman's foot is typically narrower in forefoot and heel and higher in the arch than a man's, while her calf muscle is typically lower than a man's. Fit, comfort, and performance are paramount when selecting boots. If you are a woman, ask to see women's boots. "Unisex" usually means that they won't fit as well.

car wearing them. However, they don't offer enough support to be useful for carving turns on hard snow at high speeds.

Hard Boots

Hard boots are not "hard" to use. In fact, the plastic shell on these boots provides greater leverage, power, and precision to your edging movements. Plastic boots are used by people who like to carve or race, and are becoming increasingly popular with adults who are also Alpine skiers. Hard plastic boots, however, are rarely used with freestyle boards, because the stiff boot cuff doesn't allow enough range of ankle motion for the freestyler's acrobatic maneuvers. Hard boots feature a rigid plastic shell surrounding an inner boot, usually made of leather and foam. Mountaineering or Alpine ski boots can be substituted for use with carving boards.

BINDINGS

Bindings fasten your feet to the snowboard (or is it your snowboard to your feet?). Their job is to effectively transmit the energy of your movements to the snowboard. As with boards and boots, a variety of bindings are available to match the three basic styles of riding.

Soft-Boot Bindings

Soft-boot bindings can be made of metal, plastic, or composites. Plastic bindings are a bit softer and less efficient in transmitting energy to your snowboard, and some can turn brittle when it gets really cold. As always, manufacturers seek a combination of performance, strength, durability, and lightness when constructing equipment, and bindings are no exception.

FREESTYLE BINDINGS By far the most popular type, freestyle bindings use two straps fastened over the foot to attach you to your board. These bindings perform well in a wide variety of situations, but work especially well when you want to have plenty of ankle movement,

FREESTYLE BINDINGS
Like the soft boots they hold to the board, freestyle bindings are extemely popular in the United States. Most freestyle (and soft-boot) setups are anatomically designed to specifically fit your right or left foot. Fastening levers typically buckle to the outside of the foot.

THREE-STRAP BINDINGS
The extra strap that fastens around the shin provides leverage to effect more powerful edging movements, and allows for added control and support on hard, bumpy, and chopped-up snow. Note the locking mechanism on the rear of the highback, which permits the use of the third strap – and leverage – to tilt the board on the toe edge.

LEVERAGED BOARDING

"Give me a lever and I'll move the world," said Archimedes. This principle is applied to snowboard boots and bindings, which are designed to maximize the energy transmitted from your feet to the board using leverage. The plastic cuff on a hard boot or the highback on a soft binding can be used as a lever to tilt the board on its edge. Pushing your lower leg against it adds quickness and power to your edging movements, and is particularly helpful at higher speeds and on hard snow.

HARD-BOOT BINDINGS
Used to fasten hard boots (snowboard, ski, or mountaineering boots) to the board, hard boots and bindings are popular with skiers who enter the sport. On this model, the heel is held by the wire bail and the toe is secured with the camming lever.

STEP-IN BINDINGS Step-in systems are becoming increasingly popular. Most are configured to fasten automatically when you step into them, but still require you to bend over to unfasten them manually. This system uses a bar under the forefoot that fastens to a hook on the binding, and a peg protruding from over the heel that fastens into a spring-loaded locking mechanism. There are a variety of step-in systems available, for both soft and hard boots. Like traditional strap or plate bindings, step-in systems are not designed to release in a fall.

such as when freeriding in deep powder. They are the binding of choice for freestyle in a halfpipe or terrain park. Freestyle binding systems require more muscular effort to control the board than do other binding systems, because you can't generate as much leverage by moving your lower leg against a soft boot cuff as you can against a rigid (hard) boot cuff (see "Leveraged Boarding," page 25).

THE BASELESS BINDING is a variation of the freestyle binding. Instead of having a rigid base plate, the binding straps fasten your foot directly to the top of your board. Favored by freestylers, some say the boot-to-board contact enhances their feel for the board. The downside is that baseless bindings allow less leverage than other bindings, and riders using them find it more difficult to cut hard turns at high speed.

THREE-STRAP BINDINGS These bindings feature an additional strap that fastens around your shin. Similar to a plastic boot cuff, the third strap provides additional support and leverage to tilt your board on the toe edge.

Hard-Boot, or Plate, Bindings

Good energy transmission, power, and efficiency on hard snow and at higher speeds are some of the advantages of using hard-boot bindings on a snowboard. They are typically used for high-speed carving and racing, but are becoming increasingly popular as more Alpine skiers and adults take up snowboarding. Hard-boot bindings are usually used with higher stance angles, meaning they are attached to the board on a diagonal rather than across, side-to-side (see page 30). By driving your lower leg against the boot cuffs, you can use these bindings as levers to deliver powerful edging movements to your board. Plate bindings use a camming mechanism to fasten your boot firmly into the binding.

Step-In Bindings

Manufacturers have recently come up with step-in boot/binding systems to ease entry into and exit from the rear binding. Step-ins come in a variety of configurations, and are offered in models designed to work with either hard or soft boots.

ADJUSTING YOUR GEAR

If you plan to rent equipment your first few times out, or if you are uninterested in adjusting your equipment to achieve the highest levels of performance and control, skip this section. Otherwise, grab some tools and your board and adjust it for a custom fit.

Are You Regular or Goofy?

On a snowboard, you ride with one foot behind the other. If your left foot is in front, you are "regular"; if your right foot is in front, you are "goofy." Regular and goofy are surfing terms that don't (necessarily) refer to your state of mind. Which foot should you put in front? You may already be familiar with one method used to determine your directional stance (if you don't already have a preference) — that is, to apply something with which you are already familiar to help you learn something new. For example, it can be easier to learn how to serve a tennis ball if you already know how to pitch a baseball, because they use similar movements.

CUSTOM CONFIGURING YOUR BINDINGS AND BOOTS FOR HIGH PERFORMANCE

It's astonishing how many people invest in high-performance equipment and use it "right out of the box." Most high-performance bindings and some boots have features that allow you to customize them to more perfectly fit you and your preferred riding style. Riding a performance snowboard without making these simple adjustments would be like climbing into a new car and driving off without first adjusting the position of the seat and mirrors. It'd get you down the road, but, in most cases, without the same degree of control or comfort that you'd have if you did make the adjustments. Custom configuring your equipment will allow you to more effectively ride ice and hard snow, tackle bumps, tame the steeps, carve amazing arcs, and perform in the halfpipe and terrain park. To get the most from the design of your equipment – and from your athletic abilities – take a few extra minutes to further adjust your boots and bindings. You'll find that these simple adjustments will make a tremendous difference – it's often the hidden difference that separates average riders from the really good ones!

Here are some easy adjustments that you can make to your equipment to achieve the highest levels of performance:

All boots Your boots are the important interface between you and your board, and if they do not fit well you'll sacrifice far more than comfort. A well-fitting boot will enable you to control your board using the smallest, most subtle of movements with your feet and ankles. Orthotics and footbeds custom fit the inside of your boot to the profile of your foot. Orthotics can only be made by a podiatrist; footbeds can be crafted by a trained technician at a reputable specialty ski or snowboard shop (ask around for recommendations on the best boot-fitting shop in the area).

Hard boots – canting the boot cuff People come in all shapes and sizes, and in a group you'll usually find small but significant differences in the orientation of their knees and lower legs. Some folks will be bowlegged, others knock-kneed, and still others will be in-between. Many performance

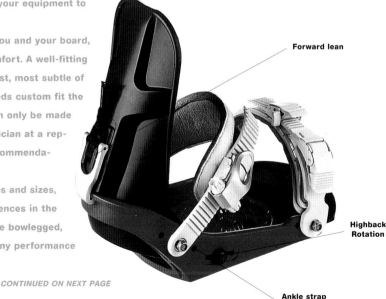

Forward lean

Highback Rotation

Ankle strap mounts

CONTINUED ON NEXT PAGE

"CUSTOM CONFIGURING" CONTINUED FROM PREVIOUS PAGE

boots have a feature that allows you to custom fit the boot cuff to the angle of your lower leg. Because it firmly holds your foot, ankle, and lower leg, and anchors you to the board in a fixed position, a supportive hard-boot cuff could actually be throwing you out of balance if you do not make this adjustment! Most boots come with a 4-degree outward lean, but your needs may be different.

The mechanism to adjust the degree of cant is usually located on the inside of the ankle joint, where the cuff joins the lower boot. Simply loosen the adjusting screw, reposition the cuff of the boot to fit the angle of your lower leg, and retighten. This allows you to feel relaxed and balanced when you stand on your board, and to edge toe-side and heel-side with equal amounts of movement.

Hard and soft boots – adjusting forward lean Leverage is the best way to create strong heel-side edging, and you can adjust the amount of forward lean on your boots or bindings to maximize heel-side edging performance. Increased forward lean makes it easier to use movements of the knee to create edging heel-side (most pros ride between 15 and 25 degrees of forward lean). This allows you to get your board on its edge without having to lean your rear end way out to the side. On the downside, a large amount of forward lean can be more tiring, because it causes you to ride lower, with a greater amount of bend in your knee. This uses your thigh muscles instead of your femur to stand against the forces generated in a turn. Also, some freestylers claim that the highback can get in the way when performing big contortions in the air. Experiment with the forward lean adjustment until you find the amount of lean that is best for your body build and preferred riding style.

Soft boots – rotating the highbacks Many soft-boot bindings have mechanisms that allow you to rotate the highback bindings so that they are parallel to the heel edge. If your bindings do, it is easy to recognize – they will have slots where the highback fastens to the base plate. If you ride with medium to high stance angles, you may want to rotate your highbacks. Simply loosen the fasteners that connect the highbacks to the base plates and reposition them by sliding them sideways along the slot until the highbacks are parallel to the heel edges. This allows you to push your lower legs against the highbacks to generate more leverage for heel-side edging.

To make your snowboard turn, you must transfer weight to your front foot. If you don't already have a clear preference, and don't have past experience on a slalom water ski, skate- or surfboard, then any other activity in which you make a weight transfer to one foot (such as serving a tennis ball, swinging a golf club or baseball bat, throwing a ball, or performing a cartwheel) will help you to fig-ure out your directional stance. You *can* learn with either foot in front, but you'll learn more quickly and easily if you determine your preferred directional stance right off.

Mounting the Bindings
Your bindings are most likely mounted to inserts built into your board. This allows you to experiment with different placements and

Soft boots – adjusting the ankle strap position Most strap bindings for soft boots offer a variety of strap positions to suit your needs. If you look along the side of your binding's base plate, you'll probably see additional holes next to where your straps fasten to it. If you do, you can reposition the ankle strap to provide you with higher performance for specific types of riding. If you reposition the strap so that it fits higher around your ankle, it'll provide you with additional leverage – and power – making toe-side edging movements. If you position the strap lower on your ankle toward your toes, it'll allow you to move your ankle more and increase your ability to contort while performing freestyle moves, although it will provide less leverage to make edging movements toe-side.

Hard boots – adjusting alignment through lifts and cants With hard boots (and some soft boots), you can also use additional lifts and cants to better align you on your board. These small, wedge-shaped shims fit underneath your bindings and are used to raise or tilt the plane of the binding to match your particular body build. (Once again, this is especially helpful with hard boots because of the rigid interface – if your boots and bindings do not conform to your particular body geometry, you'll literally be fighting your equipment to stay in balance!) Many pros have success lifting under the toes of the front binding (anywhere between 1 and and 6 degrees), and also lifting a similar amount under the heel of the rear binding. Experiment until you find the amount of lift that is right for you.

Likewise, you can adjust the amount of tilt in the plane of your binding so that you are in alignment. Canting your binding differs from adjusting the cuff cant, in that cuff canting is primarily used to fit the boot to your leg. Once your cuff is properly aligned, you can further adjust your alignment by tilting the binding to either side. The goal of canting your binding is to ensure that you are in balance and not over- or under-edged to either side. If you are underedged toe-side, you'll need to make a bigger movement to tilt the board on that edge and a smaller movement to tilt the board on its heel edge. Vice versa for being underedged heel-side. If you need to make a big movement of your body to tilt the board on its edge, you'll flounder on steeps, on ice, and in bumps.

A trained coach is your best resource to check your alignment. As with lifting, canting your bindings is dependent on your particular body build, the width of your board, and stance width and angle. You'll need to experiment to find the direction and amount of cant that is right for you.

angles for your feet, and to make quick adjustments when necessary. The following guidelines will help you to determine where (and how) to mount your bindings.

STANCE LOCATION refers to where on the board you mount your bindings.

• For a directional stance, mount your bindings 1 to 2 inches back of center (the distance from the center of the board to the center of your stance). A directional stance works best for freeriding, giving you stability at speed and more float in powder.

• For a centered stance, mount your bindings so that each is equidistant from its nearest tip. A centered stance is best if your focus is primarily spinning, acrobatic freestyle riding. This stance allows you to ride with equal ease (and abandon) in either direction, and to

COAT AND PANTS Your first layer of defense against the outside elements, coat and pants, need to be waterproof and durable.

perform balanced spin tricks.

STANCE WIDTH is the distance apart that you mount your bindings.

- Start by mounting them about shoulder width apart (17 to 19 inches between center of bindings). This distance is especially good for beginners, and is suited to the greatest variety of situations.
- Some riders like a wider stance (19 to 22 inches between center of bindings) for stability when spinning and landing airs. This stance width is primarily used for freestyle tricks. However, the board can't be bent as well around a wide stance; a dead spot is created, preventing you from using the board to its full advantage.
- Some carvers like a narrower stance (15 to 16 inches). While the board bends well using a narrow stance, it can be less stable, especially on choppy snow, ice, or bumps.

STANCE ANGLE is the angle of your feet relative to the long axis of the board. Measured from having your feet straight across the board, perpendicular to its long axis (a 0-degree stance), you must choose a stance angle that's comfortable and suited to the type of riding you'll be doing (see "Hangover: Bane of the Boarders," below). In general, you improve your balance by adjusting your rear binding to a slightly lower angle than your front binding.

- Freestylers ride low stance angles (at or close to 0 degrees) so that they can easily perform spin tricks and ride fakie.
- Freeriders choose higher stance angles (25 to 45 degrees for the front foot, 15 to 25 degrees for the back foot) because they generally ride in a forward direction.
- Carvers and racers choose even higher

HANGOVER: BANE OF THE BOARDERS

You control your speed and direction on a board by tilting it on its edge. If your boot or binding hangs over the edge of the board, it will hit the snow whenever you achieve a high edge angle and boost your edge right out of the snow, sending you on an exciting slide for life. Stance angle is best set so the toe and heel of your boot are positioned as close to the edges as possible with no overhang of either the boot or binding. This allows for effective and efficient edging adjustments. If you are blessed with large feet, you may need to rotate the bindings (after loosening the mounting turntable) and ride with a slightly higher stance angle to prevent "booting out." You can also buy an extra wide (2EEE) snowboard.

stance angles (55 to 70 degrees for the front foot, and 52 to 66 degrees for the back foot) because they ride narrow boards for quick edge-to-edge movements, and almost exclusively ride forward.

When selecting what to wear, think functional. Your garments should be durable, fit well to allow freedom of movement, and keep you warm and dry.

BOMBPROOF GLOVES
Gloves and mittens need to be both waterproof and durable. Look for double- or triple-stitched seams, reinforced palms and fingers, and wrist gaiters (which help to keep the powder outside during those epic sessions).

KEY FEATURES OF SNOWBOARD WEAR

Generous cut This allows freedom of movement and provides warmth and protection. While you don't need to go to the limits of extreme bagginess, as some riders do, choose clothes that allow you to move. A jacket shell with a long cut (down to your hips) and bibs will help keep your midriff warm and dry when fastening bindings, or on deep powder days.

Tough, breathable fabric Snowboarding can be tough on clothes, so you'll want garments that can stand up to plenty of abrasion and abuse. Look for a tough, waterproof, breathable shell.

Zippered vents Under your arms, these vents help to regulate your temperature. Open when hot; close when cool. Storm flaps covering all zippers help to keep wintry winds out. Zip-pulls (attached to zippers) allow you to open or close the vents without removing your gloves.

Reinforcement at stress points Snowboarding can be hard on clothing. Look for double- or triple-stitched seams, and reinforced material on the sides of the jacket shell, and knees and rear end of your pants. Be careful as you carry your board: Its sharp edges can cut through the stitching and material on the sides of your jacket or pants, or through your gloves.

Other Things You'll Need

Bombproof gloves Gloves take a beating when you ride. Use mittens or gloves made of strong, durable materials, that are waterproof and reinforced at the palms and fingers. Look for a long, elasticized wrist cuff to keep snow out.

Warm socks that fit Cold feet and blisters are no fun. Look for flat seams and stretchy material that doesn't wrinkle against your skin. A thin synthetic sock covered by a thicker wool or pile sock works especially well.

A hat and/or neck warmer that covers your head, ears, and neck on extremely cold days. You can lose a tremendous amount of body heat through your head: cover it, and your feet and hands will be the warmer.

Quality eyewear protects your eyes from blowing snow, harmful ultraviolet rays, and from the odd tree branch. Using eyewear with an appropriate lens tint can help to define snow and trail conditions as light changes.

Sunblock protects your face from the sun's damaging rays. Remember that snow reflects up to 90 percent of solar radiation, increasing the need to protect your skin and eyes, especially above treeline, where high altitudes and a lack of shade make sunburn an even greater threat.

Gaiters keep snow out of your boots on deep powder treks.

Heat packs for hands and feet can make the difference between riding in comfort on a very cold day and warming your frozen extremities in the base lodge. Riding is better.

RENTING OR BUYING

One of your first decisions is whether to rent or purchase your equipment. Unless you already have your own board, it's smart to rent first, and buy a board later, when you are a bit more proficient. This also allows you to try a variety of boards before you make a purchase (many shops will apply the demo price toward purchase). After you learn the basics, you'll have a much better idea of exactly what type of snowboarding you want to do, and you can then pick up a board built for that riding style. Before buying a board, you might want to attend a regional on-snow consumer demo day, where you can try cutting-edge equipment before you buy. Call manufacturers or NSAA (see the Sources section) for demo event schedules in your area.

After experiencing the fun and excitement of riding, you'll soon want to buy equipment (see the Sources section for more information on where to obtain equipment). Investing in your own gear ensures that it's always available, and is tuned and ready anytime you want to go snowboarding, including those memorable, spur-of-the-moment, call-in-sick sessions immediately after a three-foot dump. It'll also allow you to custom fit your equipment to your body type and riding style — something not all rental shops can guarantee.

How do you decide, from the hundreds of manufacturers (all of whom offer a sizable product line), exactly which board is right for you? Before you buy, ask yourself four key questions:

1. What type of riding would you like to be doing on the board? Freestyle, freeriding, and carving boards are all designed for specific types of riding. Knowing what you want to do on your board will help you to choose equipment that is right for you.

2. How much do you weigh? Boards are designed to work best within a specific weight range. If you fall outside of that range, the board will not work well for you.

3. How much do you want to spend? Boards range in price from $300 to $600, with design and materials affecting price. Know what you're paying for, and be realistic about your abilities — and needs — when selecting gear.

4. How big are your feet? "Booting out" — your boot toe or heel catching the snow when the slope gets steep or when you create a high edge angle — won't contribute to safe or fun snowboarding. Buy a board wide enough to accommodate your foot and preferred stance angle.

Work with a reputable shop. You'll get superior support and service, and knowledgeable advice from the staff. Ask friends who ride or locals for information on the best shops in your area. Good shops provide great equipment and knowledgeable, friendly service — at reasonable prices. Remember, when it comes to equipment, you get what you pay for: Saving a few dollars won't seem so smart when you're cold, lonely, and broken down on the side of the hill. You'll thank yourself a hundred times over when you invest in good gear that works.

Layering

To best adapt to the changing conditions in the mountains, and to your own levels of exertion, wear multiple layers of clothing (see "Key Features of Snowboard Wear," page 31). Layering allows you to add or remove garments as the situation demands, and helps guarantee a safe, fun, and *comfortable* snowboarding experience each time you go out. Three layers form the system.

THE INNER LAYER should cover you from head to toe. Typically made from synthetic materials such as polypropylene, the purpose of this first layer of underwear (socks, long johns, and T-shirt) is to wick moisture away from your skin and to the outer layers, where it can then evaporate, thus keeping your skin relatively dry. Wet garments that are in contact with your skin conduct 25 times more heat away from your body than dry ones. Therefore, when choosing garments for this layer, avoid cotton — it absorbs many times its weight in water and loses its insulating qualities when wet.

Base-layer garments are available in various weights to match your activity level. Use lightweight layers when it's warm or when you are really working up a sweat; medium or expedition weights when it's really cold or when you aren't exerting yourself, and thus generating little body heat.

THE MIDDLE LAYERS trap warm air next to the body. The thicker the layer of trapped air, the warmer you'll be. Two or three lightweight layers are preferable to a single heavyweight one, because you can adjust the amount of insulation you're wearing to your activity level and to fluctuating temperatures.

A rule of thumb: Shed a layer before you get totally steamed — it'll help to keep your garments (and goggles) moisture free. The same applies when temperatures drop: Add a layer before you start shivering.

THE OUTER LAYER is your protection from the elements, minimizing heat loss from wind and cold. Even the gentlest breeze can sweep away the layer of warm air surrounding your body (a process known as convection). The

LAYERING

Waterproof shell

Synthetic or down parka

Fleece jacket or vest

Synthetic or wool shirt and pants

Synthetic wicking long johns

Skin   Heat   Perspiration

BARGAIN BOARD TIPS

Shop off-season (during spring or summer) for the best prices. Many shops sell their rental and demo inventory at the end of each season to make room for next year's gear.

Look for used gear at shops, in the classifieds, or on the Web (check the Sources section for some useful home pages). Keep in mind that newer boards perform at a much higher level than older gear. It is best not to invest in any gear that is more than three years old.

Ask friends Folks who ride usually upgrade their equipment annually (new equipment makes a big difference – you'll see).

Check out early-season ski and board swaps At these preseason events, you'll find used boards, boots, and bindings at unbelievably low prices. Check out each piece of equipment carefully before buying, but realize that if you buy broken or damaged gear, you usually can't return it.

stronger the wind, the faster you lose body heat, producing a wind-chill effect that makes it feel much colder than it really is. Rain or perspiration dampens clothing, reducing its insulating properties and quickly conducting away your body's heat. Look for a waterproof, breathable outer shell that lets perspiration escape while protecting you from wind, snow, and rain.

Without a windproof, waterproof shell, you put yourself at risk for whatever weather extremes Mother Nature hurls your way.

GettingStarted
learning to control your speed and direction

GettingStarted
learning to control your speed and direction

TAKE A LESSON In the last several years, certified snowboard instructors have become common. Working with a professional will help you master the basics quickly and safely.

PREREQUISITES You've selected and adjusted your equipment, and practiced key movements inside (see "Key Movements," page 38). Now it's time to apply them on snow.

TERRAIN Find a flat, groomed, uncrowded area to practice the basic techniques. An area adjacent to a gentle groomed slope (where you'll go next) works best. Most learning areas for first-time snowboarders (and skiers) are configured in this fashion. If you're unfamiliar with the terrain, ask an instructor or patroller to point you toward the beginner's area.

GROUND SCHOOL

A would-be pilot who has never flown a plane before would not jump into the cockpit, fire up the engine, and roar off into the wild blue yonder, equipped only with the knowledge that he would like to learn how to fly. Rather, prior to his first takeoff, that person would gain a thorough on-the-ground education to learn what he needed to know to safely pilot the aircraft.

It's no different on a snowboard. You could, your first time out, head up the chairlift and try to figure out how to pilot your board down the mountain, but you would very likely crash and burn, risking injury to yourself and others. This is a painful, frustrating, and reckless way to learn.

I cannot overemphasize the value of a lesson conducted by a professionally trained and certified snowboard instructor. When combined with the information presented in this book, working with a professional snowboard instructor will help you to master the basics quickly and easily. It is the surest way to guarantee yourself a safe, fun, and *painless* first-time experience (see "Take a Lesson!," page 46, for tips on getting the most from a lesson).

After learning the basic snowboarding movements, practice them on the flats *before* employing them on a hill. Once you are com-

Text continued on page 40

BASIC STANCE You should be relaxed and comfortable as you balance on your snowboard. Remember to stand tall and to look ahead — it'll give you better balance and allow you to see where you're going.

PRACTICE AT HOME

Get a head start on high performance! Adjust gear and practice key movements inside, the night before your first lesson. Prepare a safe place to practice. A carpet or newspapers under your snowboard will prevent damage to your floor or board. Clear away nearby lamps, fragile furniture, aquariums, and priceless heirlooms. Pull on your boots, strap on your board, and practice the basic movements. With both feet fastened into the bindings, it's helpful to use a chair, door frame, or some other object for balance. Practicing indoors will prepare you well for your first time out on snow.

Key Movements

Five key movements are the foundation of good riding. The movements you'll learn on your first day out are the same ones that you'll use at whatever you choose to be your highest level of performance, be it competing on the World Cup, riding untracked powder on a heli-boarding vacation, putting up first descents on extreme backcountry routes, doing a double-black-diamond bump run for the first time, performing exciting freestyle moves in the halfpipe or terrain park, cutting high-powered arcs on a freshly groomed trail, or completing an elegant cruise down your favorite run. By focusing on these key movements, you will be well on the road to high performance from day one.

Not only do you have to be able to perform each one of these key movements, you have to be able to make and adjust all of them at the same time. As you gain skill, you refine your ability to control the timing and intensity of the movements, and to work them in varying combinations.

Upcoming chapters refer to these movements and how to apply them to ride through a wide variety of snow conditions and terrain, so it's very important that you develop a familiarity with them now.

Edging Movements

Snowboarding is, literally, life on the edge. You are almost always balanced on one of your board's two edges (toe and heel) as you ride, and must be able to tilt the board on either the toe or heel edge equally well. Edging helps you to control both your speed and direction, and will save you from nasty, body-pounding crashes. So practice edging.

Put on your board indoors and, using a chair or door frame for balance, try the following:

1. Toe-Side Edging

● Staying fairly tall, move your hips over the toe edge of your board.

● Push your knees in the same direction and lift your heels (as you would to stand on the balls of your feet) until your board is tilted on its toe edge.

● Explore the full range of edging movements, from barely tilting the board to tilting it nearly perpendicular to the floor.

● See if you can balance on the edge while tilting the board for a count of 3, then 5, then 10 seconds. Extra points if you can do this without using your hands to balance.

Not only do you need to be able to make the board tilt, you also have to be able to maintain the tilt as you ride.

2. Heel-Side Edging

Once again, stand tall. Heel-side edging movements, more than toe-side ones, change slightly with different stance angles (see page 30).

Low stance angles (feet mostly across the board):

● Tilt the board by slowly rocking back on your heels.

● Move your hips over the heel edge and straighten your knees slightly (but never fully straight – always keep them a bit bent).

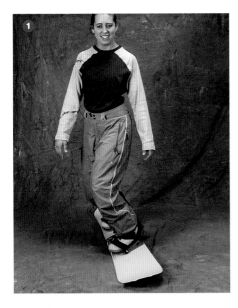

- Push down with your heels and pick up your toes.

High stance angles (toes pointed toward tip):

- Move your hips over the heel edge and tilt the board by pushing your bent knees out over the edge.
- Roll your ankles to feel weight along the little-toe side of your front foot and along the big-toe side of your rear foot.

Explore the range of heel-side edging movements and try to balance on the heel edge for extended periods as you did with the toe edge.

3. Steering Movements

These are twisting motions you make with your feet, legs, and hips to guide your board through turns. When you steer, you pivot the board around a point midway between the bindings. (In special situations – such as in the bumps, on steeps, and performing some freestyle tricks – this may change and you'll pivot around a point toward the tip or tail.) These movements work in concert with edging movements to help you control speed and direction.

As you steer, move your feet interdependently. Twist your front foot in the direction of the turn while pushing the rear foot away from the turn. Try not to push the tail out abruptly. The movement of your front foot should be complemented by the movement of your rear foot to guide the board through a round arc where the tail follows the tip.

CONTINUED ON NEXT PAGE

"KEY MOVEMENTS" CONTINUED FROM PREVIOUS PAGE

4. Fore and Aft Movements

These moves determine where along the board's length you apply most of your weight. They help you to adjust to sudden changes in the speed of your board. Fore and aft movements also can determine which end of the board heads downhill first. Shifting your weight forward encourages the tip to head downhill. Shifting it back when you are headed downhill can help to turn the tip back uphill by pushing the tail downhill. When shifting your weight, maintain an upright stance, shifting your torso without bending at the waist.

5. Flexing and Extending Your Legs

As you start moving on your snowboard, you'll encounter small (and not so small) bumps on the slopes.

Text continued from page 37

fortable with the key movements on flat ground, you'll be able to apply them more easily while in motion — first on very moderately pitched slopes, then, with more practice, on progressively steeper slopes.

Fastening the Front Foot

Having found an uncrowded flat area, fasten your front foot into the binding. Check to make sure that there's no snow stuck to the bottom of your boot or on the top of the binding. Position your foot all the way to the rear of the binding and fasten your binding. During ground school and throughout your first descents, you'll keep your rear foot out of its binding. This will save you time and energy, and allow you to practice maneuvers you'll need in order to use most lifts and to skate across flat areas. It will also help you to quickly get a feel for making key movements on

By bending your legs at the ankles and knees when going up over a bump and then extending them again as you drop down off the other side, you use your legs as shock absorbers, smoothing your ride and helping you maintain balance. Again, bend at the ankles and knees, but not at the waist; you want to maintain a balanced, upright stance and look out ahead of you.

That's it. It's that simple. If you learn how to perform these movements, you'll soon be a proficient snowboarder. Well, it's almost that simple. Actually, you need to constantly adjust these movements to work with an ever-changing mountain. You must learn to perform them in concert, yet independently of each other. For example, to ride bumps, you need to bend and straighten your legs without affecting the amount of toe or heel edge you maintain. Like the snowflakes you ride on, no two situations – or combinations – are ever exactly alike.

snow and allow you to use your free foot to regain your balance should you happen to lose it. You'll fasten your rear foot into the binding soon enough, after you've learned how to skate, glide, turn, and stop. After your front foot is fastened, make sure you fasten your safety leash.

Basic Stance

As you perform these ground-school exercises, you want to work from a relaxed, comfort-able, athletic stance. An important point: snowboarding is very much like dancing (with the mountain as your partner). Whether snowboarding or dancing, you continually move. You rarely assume — and hold — a single position. Remember: *Riding is movement*, and there is great joy in movement — especially on a snowboard. With this in mind, we'll define a good snowboarding stance as the position from which key movements are made.

When You Snowboard

STAND TALL It's more energy efficient — and easier — to support your weight with your bones than with your muscles. Try crouching down as though you were sitting in an invisible chair for an extended period to feel how hard it is to support your weight with your muscles. Then stand tall. Notice how much easier it is to carry your weight using your skeleton.

STAND IN AN ATHLETIC POSITION, with knees slightly flexed, poised to make movements.

MAKE SMOOTH, GRADUAL MOVEMENTS to maintain balance and control. You'll increase the speed and intensity of the movements as you learn.

ROUGHLY 65 PERCENT OF YOUR WEIGHT SHOULD BE ON YOUR FRONT FOOT, but you should have the ability to shift weight from one foot to the other, and from your toes to your heels.

YOUR KNEES SHOULD BE SLIGHTLY BENT, YOUR ARMS AND HANDS RELAXED, and your head upright. You'll want to stand so that you can easily make each one of the key movements.

ALWAYS LOOK IN THE DIRECTION YOU WANT TO GO.

Acclimatizing

Perform these simple maneuvers, which will get you comfortable moving with the board attached to your foot:

● Lift the board, and touch the tip and tail to the snow alternately.

● Lift your free foot and balance, one footed, on the board. Remember to look ahead, not down!

● Step off the board with your free foot and slide the board back and forth. Try this with your free foot on either side of the board.

Using the Stomp Pad

Place your rear foot on the stomp pad so that it's centered (without toes or heel overhanging the edges). It's very helpful to be able to do this *without* looking down at your feet. This move is simple, yet crucial: you'll use it on any chairlift or surface lift, and whenever you glide and stop with only one foot attached. If you have to look down to position your free foot on the board, you're *not* looking where you're going, and you increase the likelihood of falling or running into something.

Here is an exercise that will help you to use your stomp pad like a pro. Stand with your weight on your front foot and practice

ONLY YOU CAN PREVENT RUNAWAY SNOWBOARDS

Most areas have rules requiring you to use a leash to prevent runaway boards (see "The Code," page 74). A runaway board, hurtling down the hill, could strike and seriously injure someone. Although snowboard bindings are not designed to release (as do Alpine ski bindings), boards can get away — especially when you carry your board while hiking: at the halfpipe, for a favorite hit in the terrain park, or in the backcountry. Take extra care not to drop your board if you carry it while on the hill. It's a great idea to fasten the safety leash around your wrist or forearm when hiking, to guarantee that your board stays with you. If you leave your board unattended on the slope, place it across the hill, bindings down. This will help to make sure that it doesn't take an unscheduled ride without you aboard.

placing your rear foot on the stomp pad, each time making sure that your toes and heel do not overhang the edge. When you can do it consistently, fasten your seat belt, and get ready for a voyage into deep cerebral space:

1. Close your eyes and repeat smoothly stepping your rear foot onto the stomp pad.

2. Freeze each time you place your foot on the stomp pad.

3. Open your eyes to check that your foot is on the stomp pad and centered on the board. Unfreeze.

When you can perform this comfortably and consistently, without the foot overhanging the board's edges, practice stepping your free foot from the other side of the board.

Practicing Key Movements

With your rear foot centered on the stomp pad, practice the following key movements:

● Rise up and sink down. As you sink, you *flex* your leg joints (hips, knees, and ankles). As you rise, you *extend* them. Keep your upper body upright and stable.

● While standing tall, move your body toward the tip and then the tail of your snowboard. Next, using the slippery snow, push and pull your feet so the board slides backward and forward beneath you.

● Step off the board with your free foot and slowly twist your front foot back and forth to steer the board.

● Now, using your rear leg like the pencil in a protractor and your front leg like the fixed point, brush your rear foot through an arc in front of your toe edge and behind your heel edge so it leaves a smooth, round track in the snow. This duplicates the movements — and the sensations — experienced when steering the board with your bindings fastened to both feet. The action of the front foot is complemented by the movement of the rear foot to guide the board through a round, steered turn.

● Step across the board with your free foot, and tilt the board on its toe edge. Then step back across and tilt the board on its heel edge. Repeat this until you can make the movement consistently and in balance.

Toe-Side Edging

With your rear foot on the stomp pad, tilt the board on its toe edge. Do this by slowly moving your body over the toe edge, and then bending your knees in that direction. Rise up on your toes *and hold the board on edge* for a count of 3 seconds, then 5, 10, and 20 seconds.

Heel-Side Edging

When you can tilt the board consistently on the toe edge, practice tilting, and holding, the board on its heel edge. Do so by smoothly moving your body over the heel edge. With high stance angles (toes pointed toward the board's tip — typically used with hard boots), push your bent knees sideways out over the

HIGH ON BOARDING

The world record for high-altitude snowboarding is held by the late Bruno Gouvy, on Cho Oyo in the Himalayas. A pioneer of extreme snowboard descents, Gouvy snowboarded many extreme first descents, and rode the North face of the Eiger, the Dru, and the Matterhorn in a single day. He fell to his death while riding.

heel edge so the sides of your lower legs press against the cuffs of your boots. With low stance angles (toes pointed across the board — usually used with soft boots), pull your toes up toward your knees and push your lower legs against the highbacks on your bindings. Alternate practicing between the toe and heel edge.

Falling

While you probably didn't buy this book to learn how to fall, here are some hints that will help you to survive "in the unlikely event of a water landing":

● Create the ultimate learning environment: working with a qualified coach, selecting the appropriate terrain, using a sequence of progressively more challenging tasks, pacing yourself, and practicing will almost guarantee that you stay in balance, rather than wipe out.

● Practice key movements, especially edging. This, too, will ensure that you stay in balance, and will never have to suffer a humongous wipeout.

● If you feel yourself losing control or balance, fall uphill if possible. This lessens the impact.

● If all else fails and you fall downhill, try to relax and roll with the fall, rather than resist it with your arms and hands. Work with the force, not against it.

The choice is yours: If you try to rush your own learning, or if you put yourself in the hands of a well-intentioned but untrained friend, chances are good that you'll experience The SLAM. If you read — and follow — the instructions in this book, it's unlikely you'll ever suffer a painful crash.

Skating

If you've spent any time at a ski area, you've undoubtedly seen snowboarders skating across flat areas and when approaching lifts. Skating is how you get around when you have a snow-

KEEP IN MIND

Beginners find that the board tends to drift out sideways as they try to skate, particularly when they push from the toe side. If this happens to you, focus on tilting your board on its edge. A flat board can't "grip" the snow and will slide out to the side. Edging the board will allow it to grip the snow and track straight ahead.

WARM UP BEFORE RIDING

Chase your friends a few times around the base lodge to warm up before you start riding. Warming up oxygenates your blood (fueling your muscles), enhances your metabolic efficiency, lubricates your joints, and reduces the possibility of injury. You'll know you're warming up when you feel it (warm, that is) and when you start breathing hard.

Stretch out after you've warmed up. Like bending a dry twig until it snaps, stretching cold muscles increases the likelihood of injury. Shake out key muscle groups, such as the ones in your legs, torso, neck, shoulders, and arms before you start riding, or after a period of physical inactivity such as a long lift (or helicopter!) ride.

Slam-Free Snowboarding

Most people know of someone who has tried snowboarding and endured a tortuous series of painful, body-pounding falls. The fall goes by a variety of sinister and suggestive names: The Spinal Tap, The 911 Take Down, The Hospital Smash, The Hard-Pack Smack, The SLAM. It's that neck-snapping, body-crunching, edge-catch wipeout. Everyone has heard about it or seen it. Some suffer the experience and become snowboarders; some experience The SLAM and never snowboard again. The rest just live in fear of it.

Edge-catch wipeouts can hurt. Here's the worth-the-price-of-the-book-many-times-over secret to learning how to snowboard without the painful slams:

Learn edging.

That's it. Edging. Snowboarding is life on the edge. Its crucial to be able to tilt the board on its edge, and to be able to maintain the tilt. Practice this. Practice it until you can balance on the edge consistently. Then practice some more. If you allow your board to go flat on the snow, you will most likely catch an edge and slam. The spectacular slam face plant is exceeded in its sudden violence only by the dreaded, butt slam, often followed by the whiplash head smash. OUCH! You can avoid big, painful wipeouts entirely, if you are able to create — and maintain — edging on both the toe and heel edge of your snowboard. So practice it.

One other priceless bit of advice: pace yourself. Learning to snowboard is so much fun that beginners often stay out on the slope too long. If you begin to get tired but ignore the signals, you're very likely to catch an edge; your fatigued leg muscles just won't be able to hold an angle. So do pace yourself. Limit early sessions to 2 to 2½ hours, take a 30-minute break (and snack) in the lodge, and then head back to the beginner's slope refreshed.

Snowboarding has a reputation for being punishing to learn — especially on the first day. This is a myth. You can maximize your fun and minimize painful falls by developing your ability to keep your board on its uphill edge. Let the board go flat, or ride with a wavering edge, and you'll be at risk for some body-pounding falls; keep it on the appropriate edge, and you'll be smiling and bruise free at the end of the day.

board, but no hill. It's kind of clumsy, but it gets the job done.

TOE-SIDE SKATE Put weight on your front foot and push, scooterlike, with your free foot.

Start with small steps. Tilt the board slightly on its toe edge. As you skate, step no farther forward with your rear foot than your front foot. Try it first in a straight line, then in a

TAKE A LESSON!

Do yourself and everyone else on the slope a favor: take a lesson your first time out. Working with a professional instructor will maximize your fun and effectiveness. Instruction benefits everyone, from first timers to Olympic-level athletes (who train daily, year round, with skilled coaches). Most areas offer special "learn to snowboard" packages at bargain rates that usually include coaching, lift tickets, and, often, rentals. Call an area near you — or check the Web (most areas have home pages) to find out which ones offer special introductory snowboard programs.

Finding a qualified instructor How do you know that your coach has the right stuff to provide a quality learning experience? The American Association of Snowboard Instructors (AASI) offers training programs for snowboarding instructors. Certified instructors must demonstrate technical understanding and application of snowboard technique, teaching principles, and safety education. There are three levels of certification, representing excellence in the ability to teach beginning (level 1), intermediate (level 2), and advanced (level 3) lessons. To get the most from your lesson, request an AASI trained and certified instructor.

In addition to working with a professionally trained and certified snowboard instructor, there are a few things that *you* can do to get the most from your lesson:

Let your instructor know what you want Don't leave it up to chance, or the investigative skills of your instructor, to determine what you'll be learning. If you want to learn freestyle tricks in the halfpipe, tell her. If you're not sure what you want to learn, but simply want to "get better," try thinking a bit more specifically about what you'd like to do on your board.

Ask questions Don't be afraid to ask questions in a lesson. Make sure that you know exactly what your coach is asking you to do, and when, where, how, and why a particular movement works. Participate fully in each one of the maneuvers and exercises that your coach asks you to do. A halfhearted effort is a waste of your time, energy, and money.

Have fun Your participation and interaction with other members in the group will enhance everyone's enjoyment.

Practice Your coach will most likely provide you with things to practice after the lesson is over. Literally translated, this means "go snowboarding." Who could ask for a better assignment?

circle. When you feel comfortable skating, try placing your rear foot on the stomp pad after each push. See how far you can "ride the glide."

HEEL-SIDE SKATE This works better with low stance angles (toes pointed across the board). Tilt the board on its heel edge while you perform the same scooter maneuver you did with the toe-side skate.

FIGURE-EIGHT SKATE Try performing figure eights (this technique will come in handy when navigating lift-loading mazes). As you do this, push with your free foot on the side nearest the circle's center.

ALTERNATING TOE AND HEEL SKATE Alternately push from one side, then the other, in a continuous glide

Climbing

Start on a gentle hill, the one next to your flat practice area — remember? After climbing, you'll enjoy your first-ever snowboard descent, so start by climbing only a short way up. Don't make the classic beginner's mistake of climbing to the top of the hill your first time. Start low, working your way higher as you practice and gain control.

When you climb, keep your board across the hill and on its edge. Step uphill with your free foot, then step with the board.

LIVIN' ON THE FALL LINE

Anytime you snowboard, you need to be able to recognize the direction of the fall line and position your snowboard relative to it. The fall line is the straightest, most direct way down the hill — the path that a ball rolls down when you release it on a hill. The trick to stopping on a board is to feel the fall line, and to smoothly steer your board across it. If your board is across the hill and on the appropriate edge, you can easily make it stop.

That much is simple. What makes snowboarding a fascinating, ongoing challenge is that the fall line doesn't always continue in the same direction as you descend a hill. Mountains are complex: look closely at any slope and you'll see a variety of undulations — each one can affect the speed and direction of your descent. For your first snowboard rides, stick to a beginner's slope that has a simple, consistent fall line. As you progress, you'll challenge yourself by riding more complex slopes, with ever-changing fall lines.

Beginners sometimes allow their board to go flat for a moment when they're climbing. When they do this and weight their front foot, the board slides out from under them while their free foot stays put. (Ever been suspended over the water, with one foot on the dock and one on an untied boat that's slowly drifting away from it? Splash!)

Always tilt your board on edge when climbing. If you keep it edged and across the hill, it will provide you with good, solid footing. If you don't, you'll go down. 'Nuff said.

To climb toe side, position the board across the hill on its toe edge, with your free foot uphill. Step uphill with the free foot, then step with the board. Start by taking small steps. As you climb, keep your board across the hill and tilted on the toe edge. Your edged board should leave parallel tracks in the snow that look like stairs.

To climb heel side, back your way up the hill, stepping first with your free foot and then with the board. Take small steps. Remember to dig your heel edge into the snow and to keep your board across the hill.

FIRST DESCENTS
Terrain Selection

Find an uncrowded, groomed, wide beginner area with a very gentle grade. It's best to have a long, flat runout at the bottom of the hill, which allows you to get used to the feeling of gliding on the board without having to worry about how and where to stop (the board will come to a stop on the flat area). Avoid hills that end in a building, a parking lot, an interstate, or a cliff. You're looking for a gentle slope and runout space — lots of it.

The Set Up

Your free foot should be on the snow next to your board (as you practice, try this with your free foot on both the toe and heel side). With

THE TRAIL CLASSIFICATION SYSTEM AND YOU

If you're new to Alpine ski areas, you'll be relieved to know that they provide maps of their trails and facilities to help you navigate. Using a map, you'll be able to select a good area to practice, and a lift that will bring you to a beginner slope.

All slopes suitable for beginners are marked with green circles. Slopes appropriate for intermediates are marked with blue squares. You can expect to find steeper slopes, small bumps, and a variety of snow conditions on these trails. Even steeper, narrower, and bumpier trails are designated by a black diamond, and challenge experienced riders. Trails marked with double black diamonds are extremely steep, bumpy, twisty, or narrow (or some exotic and exciting combination thereof) and are for experts only. Keep in mind, however, that the designations are, to a degree, particular to each area, and that a black-diamond trail on one mountain may be quite a bit longer, or steeper, or bumpier than at another.

Ride on more difficult trails only after you can ride less difficult ones with ease. Be realistic about your abilities when selecting a trail: Although it's great to challenge yourself on more difficult terrain, choosing a trail way beyond your ability will prevent learning and encourage defensive, ineffective movements.

your weight on the free foot, point the tip of your board downhill. Don't put much of your weight on your front foot until you're ready to go — if you do, your board is likely to slide out from under you.

The Take Off

Transfer weight to your front foot as you smoothly step your rear foot onto the stomp pad (no overhang!) and balance on the board as it starts gliding down the hill. Look ahead. You don't need to push the board to get speed; allow gravity to do the work for you — it'll be easier to stay in balance.

KEEP IN MIND

People often allow their weight to fall back toward the tail of the board when they straight glide, resulting in a loss of control and, sometimes, spectacular crashes. Frequently, this occurs when beginners choose a hill that's too steep. Remember to start on the smallest hill you can find, and progress to steeper hills as you develop confidence and control. As you glide, focus on keeping your hips and torso almost directly over your front foot. This will help you to correctly distribute your weight for gliding.

GLIDING STRAIGHT Use a very gentle slope with a flat runout for your first glides. Keep your weight forward and look in the direction you're going. Allow the flat runout to bring your board to a stop. You'll find practice here to be invaluable when you take your first chairlift rides.

"YO! WATCH WHERE YOU'RE GOING!"

Here's most beginning snowboarders' number one conundrum: to maintain balance and control it's crucial to look where you want to go. Paradoxically, it's irresistible to check, visually, to see if you're doing it right. Beginning snowboarders invariably look down at their equipment to make sure that they are tilting it up on edge and steering it correctly (and, perhaps, because of the cool graphics).

It's OK – and natural – to look down, but instead try to look ahead. Looking ahead allows you to carry the weight of your head and upper body much more efficiently, and makes it easier to maintain balance. Looking ahead also allows you to spot and react to changes in snow conditions and terrain, and, most important, to cheerfully navigate around other riders, skiers, and obstacles.

TOE-SIDE TURN TO A STOP From a straight glide (1), look in the direction you want to go as you begin to steer and edge your board simultaneously (2). As your board comes across the fall line, you'll slow to a balanced stop (3) on your toe edge. Note that the upper body remains stable as the legs are steered underneath it.

The Ride!

Relax, look where you want to go, and balance over the board. Keep about 65 percent of your weight on the front foot. Ride a flat board straight down the hill (this is one of the few times when riding that you don't tilt the board on its edge). Your arms and hands should be relaxed, and in a position in which you can use them if you need to recover your balance. Balance as you glide straight down the hill. Keep your rear foot on the stomp pad and ride until the runout area brings you to a stop. Practice on this same gentle slope until you can balance comfortably on the board as it glides downhill to a stop. No tippiness. No sudden movements. Just pure, unadulterated fun. Yahoo!

If you can balance on your board on a straight glide until flat ground brings you to a stop, congratulations! You'll now be able to get off of most chairlifts with ease, because the unloading area is configured in the same way — from a gently pitched slope to a flat area.

STOPPING

If you always snowboarded on a gentle slope that runs out in a long, uncrowded flat area, you'd now know all you need to know to snowboard safely. Mountains, however, are untamed, and infinitely more fun and challenging. You'll soon progress to slopes that are steeper, narrower, or more crowded than

KEEP IN MIND

Beginners are often able to either steer their board or to bring it up on its edge, but not both. To guide a board through a round steered turn and to stop, you have to be able to make these movements *simultaneously*. Edging alone, without moving your feet to steer the board, will take you straight down the hill. Steering alone, without edging, will get your board across the hill, but you'll be at risk for a disastrous slam. Therefore, it is important to remember to steer your board and tilt it on its edge *at the same time*.

HEEL-SIDE TURN TO A STOP From a straight glide, use your legs to start the board on a round turn (1). Make smooth gradual movements, and tilt your board on its heel edge through the entire turn (2). People often overturn while trying to stop on their heel edge. Practice steering your board only enough to bring it across the fall line (3) and no farther. You'll rejoice — and be better able to arrest the steering movements of your legs — with both feet attached to the bindings.

the one you just practiced on. On these trails, you're going to need to be more than just passive, human ballast on your board. You're going to need know how to turn, slow down, and stop. Here are the basics:

Toe-Side Turn to a Stop

Use the same practice area as for straight glides. Climb a short way up the hill and set up with your tip pointing down the hill as you did for a straight glide. Your back foot is still free. Relax. This time, instead of going straight down the hill and waiting for the flat area to decelerate you, move your feet and legs to guide the board through a round, steered turn on the toe edge. To steer, twist your front foot in the direction of the turn, and push your rear foot behind you, *away* from the direction of the turn. Try to guide the board through a round arc, where the board's tail follows its tip.

If you smoothly steer and edge the board *at the same time*, it will decelerate and stop as it comes across the hill (i.e., across the fall line). As you practice these maneuvers, you'll want to be on your uphill edge. Don't allow your board to go flat, or you will slam. To go toe side, goofy riders will turn left, and regular riders will turn right.

Turning Tips

● Make smooth, gradual movements: Your track in the snow should resemble the letter "J." (If you ride goofy, it'll be a reversed looking-glass J. Don't fret, you'll get to make that sweet J soon enough — when you practice the maneuver to the heel edge.)

● As you start your turn, tilt the board up on its toe edge *and keep it there through the entire turn*, until after you come to a stop, with your board across the hill and you, the wily navigator, in perfect balance.

● Resist the temptation to peer down at your board's astonishingly cool graphics. Keep your head up. Look toward where you want to go.

● Approximately 65 percent of your weight should be on your front foot.

● Remember, you steer your board by moving both feet. The movement of the front foot is enhanced by the rear one — and vice versa.

● Guide the board in a trajectory where the tail of the board follows the tip; don't abruptly kick the tail across the hill.

Heel-Side Turn to a Stop

When you can come to a stop consistently and in balance on your toe edge, try the same maneuver on your heel edge to turn in the opposite direction. Look where you want to go, steer the board using smooth, gradual movements of your feet and legs, and tilt the board on its heel edge as you steer it across the hill. Try to come to a stop in perfect balance, then step off the board with your rear foot.

TWO ARE BETTER THAN ONE With only one foot attached in the binding, many begin-

ners overturn on their heel edge. They are able to guide the board through a beautiful, round, steered trajectory, but instead of being able to stop turning when the board comes across the hill, their board continues to turn so that the tip ultimately points up the hill, and they become hapless human cargo, experiencing a thrilling, though unintentional, backward freestyle ride.

This happens because their rear foot is not yet fastened into the binding, and can't transmit powerful steering and edging movements to the board. Think of your board as one of those giant hook-and-ladder fire engines that is so long that it has a steering wheel in the back to guide the rear wheels. The combined action of both steering wheels enables the truck to be navigated around tight city blocks. Similarly, when your rear foot is fastened into the binding, it works to guide the tail of your snowboard. You can use it to arrest the turn-

TIGHT IS RIGHT

Your boots and bindings transmit your movements (energy) to the board. For high performance, and to prevent bone-crunching slams your first day out, it's important that your boots and bindings be sized and adjusted to fit you.

Use snowboarding boots, not pac boots, hiking boots, cowboy boots, work boots, high tops, ballet shoes, or birkenstocks. Snowboarding boots are designed specifically for riding, and will provide comfort, warmth, and support. Don't borrow equipment from your friends — unless it fits you perfectly and is correctly adjusted. To ensure a good transmission of energy, note the following:

● Make sure your boots fit your feet, and that they are laced or buckled securely. Your foot should not move around or lift up inside the boot.

● The boot should be comfortable and supportive.

● As you fasten your foot in the binding, make sure it is all the way to the rear, and that there isn't any snow between the boot and the binding.

● Fasten the binding tight — so there is no movement of the boot in the binding.

Snug-fitting boots and bindings will give you the most effective energy transmission to your board, enhancing responsiveness and making turning and stopping much easier. Always remember: "If it ain't tight, it ain't right!"

ing motion, so that your tail does not wash out (skid downhill) on the heel-side turn.

But since your rear foot isn't yet fastened into the binding, performing this maneuver is not possible. You can, however, gain control as you turn to a stop on your heel edge, by slowing down and putting a bit more weight on your rear foot. Rejoice in the fact that turning and stopping are going to be much easier when you fasten your rear foot into the binding. But for now, keep it unfastened, and stay on the smaller hills.

You've been keeping your rear foot unfastened as you practice (and will for a wee bit longer still) for three reasons:

1. It helps prevent slams by enabling you to step off with your rear foot if you need to catch your balance.

2. It makes your first lift experience a happy one because you ride most lifts with only one foot attached.

3. It saves energy: Fastening and unfastening your rear foot can burn some serious calories.

However, riding with your rear foot unfastened does not allow you to steer or edge the board as effectively as with both feet attached.

When you ride this way you simply have less control. That's why you never see anyone freeriding down the mountain with only one foot attached, and why it's important for you to ride with one foot fastened *on very gentle slopes only*.

Traversing the Slope

So far you've been riding straight down the hill, learning to control your speed and direction. Now you'll learn about a tool that you can use anytime to tame the meanest, steepest, most unforgiving slope on the mountain.

What is it? Dynamite? A bulldozer?

Nope. It's a traverse.

A traverse is a diagonal descent across the slope. Because you go across the hill, you're able to go as slow — or as fast — as you want. You choose how far down the hill you want to steer your board: The farther you go down the hill, the faster you go. The more you go across the hill, the slower you go. The amount that you steer the board down the hill is called your *angle of attack*.

It's a wonderfully useful thing to know how to traverse because it can make any slope

FIVE STEPS TO A SOLID TOE-SIDE TRAVERSE

1. Climb the gentle slope you've been riding. (Are you getting warm yet?) Regular riders will be traversing the hill to the right; goofy riders to the left. Plan your climb accordingly.

2. This time, as you prepare to ride, point the tip of your board diagonally across the hill. Remember to keep your weight on the free foot and your board on edge as you position the snowboard.

3. *Keeping your board on the toe edge,* step your rear foot onto the stomp pad (no overhang).

4. Hey! This should seem familiar. It's the same thing you practiced earlier, only you're starting off edged and with the board already steering partway across the hill. Look where you want to go, relax, and ride the board almost all the way across the slope. Remember to give yourself room to stop — you don't want to explore the woods on the side of the trail, do you?

5. To stop, finish steering the board until it comes completely across the hill. Remember, keep it on its edge the whole time.

LOADING THE CHAIRLIFT Keep your tip pointed forward and lift your free foot as you load a chairlift.

conditions, such as ice, that make controlling your speed difficult. Traversing is your ace in the hole when the mountain throws something gnarly at you.

Practice traversing the hill on the toe edge. When you get to the far side of the trail, step off your board and position it so it points in the other direction diagonally across the trail. Your free foot should be uphill and your board now tilted on the heel edge. When you're ready, relax and repeat the maneuver on the heel edge. Try to make a series of smooth traverses and stops in balance, working your way down the slope.

When you can straight glide, traverse, and stop in balance on both edges (all of which takes the average beginner less than two hours to achieve), congratulations! You've completed ground school — and are ready for the lift.

USING LIFTS

Although Alpine skiers will be familiar with using lifts, there are some particulars to keep in mind when using a snowboard, so even if you ski, don't be tempted to skip this section.

Use a map (or ask a ski instructor) to locate the lift that services trails most appropriate for beginners. Before attempting to ride the lift, watch other snowboarders using it. If you have any questions or concerns, mention to the lift attendants that it's your first time. Often they're able to slow the lift to help beginners get on. They are trained to help you and are usually very happy to do so.

Chairlifts

The chairlift — by far the most common type of lift in the world — is simple to use on a board, once you get the hang of it.

on the mountain less steep. You never *have* to go straight down the hill.

Traverse whenever you find yourself on a slope that is so steep it makes you uncomfortable, or whenever you encounter snow

UNLOADING THE CHAIRLIFT Place your free foot on the stomp pad and point your tip forward before you touch down. As you stand, keep your weight forward and anticipate a very slight acceleration as you begin to glide down the ramp. After you stop, skate out of the unloading area, allowing those behind you plenty of room to get off.

LOADING

1. Skate into the loading area (this is typically marked with a line or with orange cones). Keep your tip pointing forward. Whenever you are in a loading or unloading area, be very alert for oncoming chairs.

2. Look over your shoulder to watch for the chair as it comes around the wheel. Sit in the chair as it comes underneath you. Keep your tip pointing forward until you're off the ground.

3. Many beginner lifts hang low to the ground so that they can be used by small children. As you sit, be careful not to let your rear leg get caught underneath a low-hanging chair. Swing your free foot ahead of you and hold it there until you're clear of the loading area.

Remember, the tip of the snowboard must be pointing straight ahead (in the direction that the lift is taking you) whenever you load or unload a chairlift. Don't allow your board to turn to the side in the process of sitting down or you may catch an edge and get

Two problems often surface with beginners getting off chairlifts:

1. They don't put their rear foot on the board until after they start gliding down the ramp. When they finally remember to put it on the board, they often miss the stomp pad — or their foot is hanging halfway off the board. That makes it far more difficult to stay in balance or control the board, and you'll often see novices face down on the unloading ramp or crazily hopping on their free foot trying to catch up with their board. You can be spared this indignity because you know to put your foot on the stomp pad *before* you touch down.

2. They fail to anticipate the slight increase in speed that accompanies gliding down the unloading ramp, letting their boards accelerate out from underneath them as they get off the chair. Invariably, they fall over backward. When you unload, expect to *glide*. Ride the glide. Remember to keep your weight forward (approximately 65 percent on the front foot) and look ahead as you get off the chair.

RIDING A SURFACE LIFT Hold onto the lift handle and lean back slightly to counterbalance the force pulling you up the hill. Keep your tip pointed forward and stay in the track while balancing over your board. After you feel comfortable riding the surface lift, experiment by putting the handle behind your front leg.

smooth, gradual steering movements to guide their boards through round turns. You can learn a lot by studying other riders.

UNLOADING

1. As you approach the unloading area, raise the safety bar, point your tip forward, and slide your rear end toward the edge of the chair. Your hands should be on the edge of the chair, ready to gently push off from it as you stand.

2. Place your rear foot on the stomp pad (no overhang) *before* your board touches the snow.

3. Stand up tall and balance over your board when you get to the unloading zone. Look ahead. Keep your weight on your front foot and anticipate a slight acceleration as you begin to straight glide down the ramp.

4. Come to a stop and skate well clear of the unloading zone. Now you're ready to ride!

Surface Lifts

Surface lifts include T- and J-bars, pomas, and handle- and rope-tows. These lifts pull you uphill along a prepared track in the snow. They are great for a beginner, because you get to snowboard 100 percent of the time — developing your skills as you use the lift. In addition, many surface lifts allow you to get off partway up the hill if you're uncomfortable riding to the top. If possible, ride alone your first few times up.

When using a surface lift, *always* keep your tip pointing forward and ride in the track. Steering to the outside of the track could derail the lift. Practice your turns on the way down, not up, the hill.

LOADING

1. Skate into the loading area. Keep your tip pointing up the hill.

2. Weight your free foot, especially if the

yanked right off the chair, risking public humiliation or worse. Keep your tip pointing forward!

RIDING THE LIFT

1. While riding the lift, swing down the safety bar (if there is one). Place your board on the footrest (if there is one). Enjoy scintillating conversation with your friend (if you have one).

2. If your chair does not have a footrest, help to support the weight of your board by positioning your rear foot behind your front foot's ankle, or under the heel edge of the board.

3. Watch for other snowboarders on the slope. They may help to preview some of the maneuvers you'll practice on your ride down. See if you can identify which edge they're on (if they're not on an edge, you'll be treated to a spectacular wipeout). Watch them make

loading area is not flat. This lets you stand still in the loading area, rather than unintentionally sliding backward.

3. Look behind you, and grab the T-bar or poma handle as it passes you.

4. When you grab the lift, take a few skating strides with your free foot — pushing the board along the track — before you place it on the stomp pad. This will get you going at about the same speed as the lift and help prevent you from being pulled over the tip of the board.

RIDING THE LIFT

1. Hang on, and get pulled like a water-skier. Keep your arms bent, and ready to work like shock absorbers to smooth your ride.

2. Stand tall, not bent over at the waist, and look ahead. You'll need to lean back ever so slightly to counterbalance the force pulling you uphill.

3. Balance on the board as you steer it to keep it in the track.

KEEP IN MIND

When loading surface lifts, beginners often get yanked forward, right over the tips of their boards and onto their faces. This can be embarrassing if it happens repeatedly in front of a long lift line. It happens because novice boarders don't take skating steps as they grab the lift handle. As you grab, remember Sir Isaac Newton and one of his greatest hits — the First Law of Motion: When you're at rest (ready to load), you'll tend to stay at rest until acted upon by a force (the lift). Don't let that force pull you off balance. Anticipate it, and work with it, by taking some skating steps. Then, you'll always load and ride the lift in balance.

4. If you lose your balance, you can often recover by taking some skating steps.

5. If you fall, get out of the track as quickly as possible. Ride back down (the slope, *not* the track) to the loading area.

6. If the lift stops while you're riding, step off the board with your free foot so that you don't slide backward down the track. Don't forget to take those skating steps as the lift starts up again.

UNLOADING

1. When you get to the unloading zone, let go of the lift handle.

2. Keep your weight on your front foot as you glide down the ramp. Keep your rear foot on the stomp pad.

3. Quickly skate out of the unloading area. Give the people coming up behind you plenty of room to get off.

Trams and Gondolas

These types of lifts are relatively straightforward. You walk on and off the lift, with your board off. Gondolas often have a holder outside the cabin in which to carry your board. If you're unsure how to use it, ask the lift attendants.

If you carry your board onto a lift, whether tram or gondola (as well as on shuttle buses), be courteous. Carry the board in front of you, vertically, so that it doesn't hit anyone or take up a lot of space. Be careful with sharp edges and wet boards, especially in close quarters. You wouldn't want to slash someone's clothing or get them wet. Hold onto your board so that it doesn't fall over and strike a fellow skier or boarder on the lift. Be prepared to answer a multitude of questions from people who might like to try snowboarding. Spread the word.

STANDING UP HEEL SIDE Starting with your board down across the hill (1), use your rear hand to push yourself off the snow (2). Pull that hand closer to the board (3), which transfers your weight to your feet and positions you over the board, allowing you to stand up on your heel edge (4).

Fastening the Rear Foot

OK, you're at the top of the lift and have skated to an uncrowded area on a wide, well-groomed, gently pitched beginner's slope. Although you know how to fit your front foot into the binding, fastening your rear foot into the binding is decidedly different. What seemed to be self-evident and simple is actually a bit demanding. Take a moment, and your first experience will be a positive one.

First, select a site. If you have soft boots and bindings, look for a handy bench. Increasingly, areas are providing them as a dry, comfortable place for snowboarders to fasten bindings. If you can't find a bench, choose a spot where you have plenty of room on either side; not immediately next to the lift or to trees. Sit down on the snow, facing downhill (this is why waterproof pants are a great idea when first learning to snowboard). Fasten your rear foot into the binding. As when fastening your front foot, check to make sure that there's no snow stuck to the bottom of your boot or on the top of the binding. Position your foot all the way to the rear of the binding and fasten it tight.

When you sit on the snow on a ski area slope, you are in a vulnerable position. Being low on the snow, you're difficult to see from above. You're facing downhill, so you won't see boarders and skiers coming from above, and it's hard to move quickly from this position to avoid someone out of control. Finally, all of your vital organs are located at snow level, where a fast-moving, out-of-control ski or snowboard could cause serious injury.

Therefore, whenever you sit in the snow, whether to fasten your rear foot into the binding or while waiting for your friends, keep safety in mind. Choose a place that's highly visible, and away from traffic. You want to be able to be seen from above, so oncoming skiers and snowboarders can navigate around you, not over or through you (see "Where Not to Sit," below).

Standing Up
PREREQUISITES

1. Start uphill from your board — that way, you'll automatically tilt the board on the appropriate uphill edge as you stand up.

2. Position the snowboard exactly across the hill before you try to get up. Do not let it stray from this position as you stand. If your board is not exactly across the fall line, it will begin sliding as soon as you try to stand. You'll probably be moving alarmingly fast by the time you finally stand up.

3. Dig your uphill edge in. With the board across the hill and tilted on its uphill edge, you won't move until you want to.

4. Check uphill before you start to make sure that you don't cut anybody off.

STANDING UP TOE SIDE This is much easier than standing up on your heel edge. To do so, however, you need to master the flip. This is one of the most delightfully awkward movements in all of snowboarding.

1. Roll over, sideways, from a sitting to a kneeling position.

2. As you roll, lift up both feet and roll in the direction of the tail of your snowboard. You'll find it's very easy to stand from the resulting kneeling position.

STANDING UP HEEL SIDE This requires some abdominal strength and flexibility.

1. Sit uphill from your board, which is across the hill. Dig your heel edge in.

2. Bend your knees, with your hips and rear end as close to the board as is comfortable.

3. Hold onto your toe edge with your rear hand. Use it to *pull* yourself over the board as you stand up. This also helps to keep your heel edge dug in.

4. Put your front hand on the snow just a bit behind your front hip. *Push* yourself up with this hand as you stand.

5. Get your weight over the board quickly *before* you stand. To do this, slowly slide your front hand closer to your board. This will transfer whatever weight you're supporting with that hand to the board.

6. Keep your board on edge and across the hill throughout the process. Check uphill, and prepare for action.

THE MOMENT OF TRUTH

With both feet attached to the bindings, you'll now enjoy an even greater ability to control your speed and direction on your snowboard. Keep in mind, however, that you'll no longer be able to step off of the board with your rear foot should you need to regain your balance. It's crucial, at this stage, that you are able to edge and steer the board in balance. These key

WHERE NOT TO SIT

Do *not* sit on the snow in these areas:

High-traffic areas

    Lift loading/unloading areas

    narrow trails, and catwalks

    In the middle of an intersection

    Under a jump

Where you can't be seen from above

    Under a knoll or steep transition

    Under a jump

    On the downhill side of a tight corner in the trail

Where things can fall out of the sky onto your head

    Under a chairlift

    Under a jump

HEEL-SIDE SIDESLIP Keep your board across the hill and always tilted on the appropriate edge. The sideslip gives you speed control: It can be used anytime you get into a demanding situation, such as a super-steep slope or "weird" snow (see Chapter 10). It's your snowboarding ace in the hole.

To become proficient at controlling your speed and direction on the board (and to develop the skills necessary to make turns) practice the following techniques:

Toe-Side Traverse

After you fasten your rear foot into the binding, and before you stand up, roll over on the snow so that you are in a kneeling position. You should be uphill from your board and it should be across the hill. Check up the hill and stand up, balancing on your toe edge. Relax, look in the direction you want to go, and shift weight to your front foot. Move your feet and legs to steer the board's tip slightly down the hill. Keep your angle of attack low: go mostly *across* the hill. To stop, smoothly twist your front foot in the direction of your turn and push your rear foot down until your board is across the hill again. As you do so, tilt the board higher on its edge. Your upper body should be oriented in the direction you're traveling (across the hill) as you make the steering movements with your feet and legs. If your practice trail is wide, try stopping several times on your toe edge as you work your way across the slope. When you get to the edge of the trail, come to a stop, and kneel down on the snow to give thanks to the universe.

Once you develop skill in traversing and stopping on your toe edge, steer your traverse farther down the hill each time. You'll now want to traverse the trail in the other direction. From a kneeling position on the snow, flip over to stand up on your heel edge.

Heel-Side Traverse

As you stand up on the heel edge, relax. Shift your weight to the front foot as you smoothly steer the tip of your board down the hill a lit-

movements will help you to control your speed and direction during your first ride with both feet attached. If you haven't yet perfected the steering and edging movements so that you can glide to a stop on either edge in balance, continue practicing. Otherwise, you'll suffer some serious wipeouts.

tle. Once again, keep your angle of attack low until you feel comfortable and in balance as you traverse the slope. Make smooth, gradual movements to steer the board back across the hill to skid to a balanced stop. When you get to the far side of the trail, change to your toe edge using the flip (see "Standing Up Toe Side," page 59). Practice on both the toe and heel edge until you can traverse the slope, control your speed and direction, and stop at will, remembering always to keep the uphill edge of your board dug into the snow.

Sideslips

TOE SIDE AND HEEL SIDE When you're able to control your speed and direction traversing on your toe and heel edge, try sideslipping. Sideslipping is guiding your board so that it skids sideways down the hill on its uphill edge (with no forward movement at all). Like traversing, sideslipping can be used when you feel overly challenged by terrain or snow conditions. If you master the sideslip, you'll always have a safe way to descend *any* slope in control, from mellow, green-circle beginner trails to impossibly steep double-black-diamond chutes. It's your snowboarding ace in the hole, so practice it.

1. Start on your toe edge with the board across the hill.

2. Keep your weight equally distributed between your feet.

3. Now, while keeping the board across the hill, gradually reduce the amount of edging. You'll start sliding sideways, down the fall line.

4. See if you can sideslip for a count of three, then increase the edging to bring the board to a stop.

When you can sideslip for a three count and stop consistently, increase the count to 5,

10, 15, and so on. See if you can maintain a constant speed as you sideslip the slope. Focus on keeping your weight evenly distributed between your feet, and steering the board so that it remains across the fall line. Practice on both the toe and heel edges (flip to change edges) so that you can sideslip and stop consistently on either edge.

VARIABLE-SPEED SIDESLIPS You're now going to give yourself a transmission. You'll have four gears, with first being the slowest speed at which you can sideslip, and fourth, top sideslipping speed. As you sideslip, challenge yourself to smoothly shift gears from first to second, back to first, then to third, and fourth. When you hit any gear, pause and ride at that speed for a count of five before shifting gears.

This develops your ability to adjust the edge angle to achieve a desired speed. Practice until you can consistently perform sideslips at a variety of speeds on either edge, *without* catching your downhill edge and slamming.

Falling Leaf

After traversing and sideslipping, and learning to read the ever-changing fall line, you're ready for freestyle! Here's a fun beginner freestyle move that gives you even more control.

At the end of a traverse across the slope, instead of rolling on the snow or jumping to get on your other edge (how déclassé), stay on the same edge and ride *backward* (fakie) across the hill, standing the entire time. Imagine, after you learn this you'll be able to go in either direction, on either edge. Here's how:

1. On your toe edge, traverse the slope.

2. As you slow to a stop at the far side of the trail, look back over your rear shoulder, shift your weight to your rear foot, and steer the

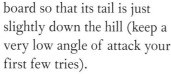

board so that its tail is just slightly down the hill (keep a very low angle of attack your first few tries).

3. Stay on your toe edge the whole time.

4. Slowly start gliding in the other direction, riding backward on the snowboard.

5. Smoothly steer the board back across the hill to stop.

This basic freestyle move is known as the falling leaf maneuver. Ride backward slowly across the slope, slowing to a stop on the far side of the hill by steering across the hill and edging. Then steer your tip back down the hill a little to cut back across the hill going forward. Your descent will be a connected series of traverses and reverses, going forward and fakie, on a single edge.

Remember to make ultrasmooth, gradual movements to keep the board on its edge the whole time, and to keep your angle of attack low until you are able to go forward and fakie

FALLING LEAF (HEEL SIDE) Traverse the slope on your heel edge (1), keeping your angle of attack low for speed control. When you get to the edge of the slope, steer the board across the hill (2) by pushing your rear foot slowly down the hill to further slow down. Continue pushing your rear foot to steer the tail of the board slightly down the hill (3) while you transfer weight to that foot to traverse the slope fakie (remember to keep your angle of attack low for speed control). Look in the direction you want to go (4). When you get to the far side of the trail steer the tip of your board back down the hill (5) to slow down again. Like the sideslip, the falling leaf, or reverse traverse, can get you out of a jam – so practice it!

in control at gradually higher speeds. With a little practice, you'll feel as much control and confidence going backward as forward. This is good, because knowing how to perform the falling leaf can get you safely down any steep slope in style and in control of your speed and direction.

GARLAND TURNS (TOE SIDE) These are small, scalloped turns that you can make as you traverse the slope. From a stop with your board across the hill and on the appropriate edge (1), steer the tip of your board slightly down the hill (2,3) using smooth, gradual movements of your legs. Before you gather too much speed (do not point your board down the hill, you're still traversing here, OK?), guide the board back across the hill so that you slow to a near stop (4–6). Repeat until you get to the edge of the slope. Focus on making a series of small, round curves as you traverse. At the slope's edge, switch edges and repeat.

Practice on both the toe and heel edge until you feel confident and in control. Explore going all the way across the slope, then try a series of quick direction changes on the same edge. See if you can navigate around objects on the slope. Explore increasing your angle of attack. Combine the falling leaf with variable-speed sideslips to develop your skills.

Garland Turns

Garland turns are a series of partial turns across the hill without edge changes. Practice them on a wide, uncrowded slope.

1. As you did in a traverse, weight your front foot as you steer the tip of your board slightly down the fall line, then back across the hill so you slow down. Make the steering movements with your feet and legs; your upper body should be stable, and facing across the slope.

2. Before you stop, steer the tip slightly down and across the hill, and across again, staying on the same edge the entire time. Repeat.

3. Try to connect a smooth series of garland turns across the hill.

4. When you get to the far side of the slope, flip over and practice on the other edge.

5. Focus on steering the board through a round turn using movements of your lower body. The tail of the board should follow the tip. As you develop proficiency, increase your angle of attack. Explore making huge, swooping turns, or smaller, quick ones.

6. When you're comfortable with forward garlands, try them fakie!

Mastering this useful and fun move is your last step before making full turns across the fall line. In traversing and sideslipping you've learned the middle and finish of the turn. The garland lets you practice the initiation of a turn as well. After familiarizing yourself with all of the parts of the turn, making the whole turn for the first time will be a lot easier.

FirstTurns

developing confidence and rhythm

4

developing confidence and rhythm

break it down into four parts: the preparation, the initiation, the middle, and the finish.

You've already learned three of those parts: traverses and garlands have allowed you to practice the preparation, initiation, and finish of a turn. As you increase your angle of attack, you will begin to practice the middle of the turn, in which you make the switch from toe edge to heel edge (or vice versa) as you cross the fall line.

BASIC TURN
PREREQUISITES

● You are comfortable and have good balance whether the rear foot is in or out of the binding. No waving arms, stiff legs, leaning back when in motion, or tipping to the sides.
● You can perform a straight glide to a stop on both toe and heel edge in balance.
● You can traverse on the toe and heel edge in balance with speed control.
● You can sideslip and stop on both edges in balance.
● You can perform the falling leaf, controlling both your speed and direction on either edge.
● You can perform garlands on both edges with speed and direction control.

TERRAIN Make your first turns across the fall line on a very gentle, wide, well-groomed slope. If there are others using the slope, wait for a lull in the traffic; you'll appreciate having plenty of room and no distractions as you

In snowboarding, as in politics and cooking, timing is everything. Knowing when and where to perform a particular move often makes the difference between a wipeout and balanced snowboarding. To give you a clearer understanding of the timing of a turn, we'll

1. Beginners often move to their new edge too early in the turn, especially when turning from the heel to the toe edge. This usually results in their falling to the inside of the turn. Avoid this by timing your edge change to occur at or around the fall line. Do not move to your toe edge until the middle of the turn. As always, make smooth, gradual movements to steer and to change edges; this will increase the likelihood of maintaining control and balance.

2. Novices try to make their first turns on the steeper parts of the beginner slope. Keep in mind that although a slope is rated for beginners, it is comprised of steeper and gentler sections. Although the speed that accompanies pointing your board down a steep section of the hill can be exciting (or terrifying, depending on your point of view), boarding too early on terrain that is too steep encourages defensive movements, such as moving weight onto your rear foot, or pivoting the board hurriedly across the slope, rather than steering the board through a round turn. Start with easier slopes, and as you develop consistency, make your turns on progressively steeper sections of the beginner trails.

make your first turns.

Remember, snowboarding is life on the edge. To link turns down the slope, you'll need to change edges from toe to heel and back again as you connect your turns. Practice smoothly rolling the board from one edge to the other while waiting on the lift line, and on any convenient flat spot. Practice until you can do it consistently. The timing of this edge change — where you smoothly roll the board from one edge to the other — is crucial.

Turn Across the Fall Line

1. Weight your front foot.

2. Look toward where you want to go.

3. Use your feet and legs to steer the board through a round turn. Twist your front foot in the direction and push your rear foot away from the direction you want to turn. Make smooth gradual movements.

4. Make a smooth edge change at or around the fall line, by rolling the board from one edge to the other.

5. Finish the turn, steering all the way across the hill for speed control. Stay on your new edge.

Focus on one turn at a time, rather than immediately trying to link them. After you turn, ride a long traverse and look for a good place for your next turn. Remember to control your speed by skidding, and also by steering the board across the hill

1-2

3

4

5

1-2

PARTS OF A TURN
Knowing the parts of a turn will help you to make moves at exactly the right time. Knowing when and where to move can make the difference between a successful descent and a bone-crunching fall.

BASIC TURN This is the first time you'll make an edge change during a turn and its timing is crucial. Weight your front foot and smoothly steer the tip of the board through a round arc (1). Look where you want to go. In the middle of your turn, make a smooth edge change (2); if you make it any earlier, you'll fall. Continue steering the board through a round arc on your new edge (3), remembering to slow down by steering all the way across the hill (4). After you've controlled your speed and when conditions permit (gentle slope, no traffic), start your next turn.

PREREQUISITES You are able to control your speed and direction down a beginner slope, and are comfortable performing skidded traverses (and reverses), sideslips, garlands, and basic turns. You're ready to link your turns together in an uninterrupted series as you descend a variety of beginner trails.

Linked Turns

As you gain control and confidence you'll begin riding faster, and you'll venture beyond tame beginner slopes. You'll begin to encounter bumps (or moguls) — some small, some not so small. If you're unprepared for them, they can send you flying. This is where your suspension system comes in: Use your legs like shock absorbers, flexing and extending them to work with the forces generated by speed and bumps.

While waiting on the lift line, practice sinking and rising over your board. When you sink, bend your ankles, knees, and hips, but don't bend over at the waist. Keep your upper body erect. Explore the range of possible movement: get as low, then as tall, as you can. Mastering the timing and the intensity of flexing and extending will help you link turns and ride at higher speeds

(this is called finishing your turn). Try to descend the entire beginner slope in balance, alternately turning and traversing the whole way down. If the trail has steep, narrow, or crowded sections, use maneuvers you're familiar with (traverses, reverses, sideslips, and garlands) until you return to terrain and conditions suitable to making turns.

LINKED TURNS Add a bending and extending movement of your legs to help you effortlessly link turns together. Bend your legs through the middle to the end of your turn (1). Rise to start your next turn (2), and sink again through the middle to the end of your next turn (3). Bending and extending your legs also helps you to develop a suspension system, which is invaluable in riding at higher speeds and on a variety of terrain and snow conditions.

on an enormous variety of snow conditions and terrain.

Practice this movement at the top of the lift as well. Then try it in motion, while traversing the hill. Keep your speed in control as you descend across the slope, rising and sinking over your board. See if you can flex and extend and still maintain the same amount of edge angle. Try to maintain a constant speed as you flex and extend through a series of traverses. As you gain confidence, try extending so quickly that you make the board light, then try jumping and landing in balance as you traverse. Practice on both toe- and heel-side traverses.

Next, incorporate flexing and extending into your turns. Rise up during the start of your turn, then sink down during the middle through the end of your turn. Traverse the slope in a slightly flexed stance and then extend again to start your new turn. Rising to start your turn makes it easier to steer, because you reduce the amount of weight on

Beginners often find themselves overturning (turning so far that the board begins to head uphill) on their heel-side turn. This can happen when you put too much weight on your front foot, or when you push your rear foot too far down the hill while completing the turn (or both).

If you find yourself overturning on your heel edge, put a little more weight on your rear foot through the finish of the turn to keep the board's tail from "washing out," or sliding too far down the hill.

Practice the finish of a heel-side turn by doing a series of garlands on the heel edge. Focus on making smooth steering movements with your legs to guide the board through a curved trajectory, and not pushing the rear foot (and with it the tail of the board) too far down the hill before you start your next garland.

CORRIDOR Envision a straight, wide corridor going down the middle of a slope and make your turns within it. Leave yourself space on the outside of the corridor just in case you can't quite pull off the turn in time. Progress to increasingly narrower corridors.

STRAIGHT LINE Envision a straight line going down the middle of the slope and make symmetrical turns on either side of it. Progress from long to short turns.

OBSTACLE COURSE The object is to go around a series of obstacles on a wide, gentle slope (ski schools frequently create obstacle courses on the beginner area). It can be as fun – and as challenging – as you want to make it. Note: Do not blithely go through race courses that have been set up on the hill without first checking with the coach. You could get mowed down by the athletes who are training there.

the board. It can also help you to transition into your next turn. The sequence, then, is rise to turn, and sink through the finish. Repeat. Again. And again *ad delerium*.

GETTING RHYTHM

There are many approaches to developing rhythm in your turns. You'll immediately know you've got it when you're doing it. You'll begin to use the energy of one turn to lead you into the next, and your turns will happen one after the other in a delightful series down the hill. Yahoo! This is where the fun *really* begins! Some tips to attaining rhythm:

● Envision a corridor and make turns within that passageway. Divide the wide slope on which you've been practicing in half, and use the middle of the slope to allow yourself an "out" if you don't make your turn in time. Ride the wide corridor and work toward progressing to narrower corridors.

● Find or envision a straight line down the hill and make turns that are symmetrical on either side of it. Check your tracks, if you can see them, for accuracy.

● Counting is a good way to establish a rhythm. "Turn-two-three, turn-two-three" will help your riding (and your waltz).

● Ride around cones, shadows, or other

objects on the slope. Use the obstacle/slalom courses, set up by the ski school, on beginner hills.

● Follow someone who is making linked turns on her snowboard and turn when she does, allowing her to help you establish a rhythm. Remember: no rear-end collisions; maintain a safe distance!

● Let your breathing be your cue. Inhale as you rise to start a turn, exhale during the middle through the end of the turn.

● Ask a friend to be a pencil, drawing a curved line as he links long turns down the hill. Your job is to be Marvin the Human Eraser: Try to ride over his track, erasing it.

● Have a friend ride down the beginner hill and work as Turn Controller. Ask her to move her arms like those people who help to park airplanes, pointing alternately and rhythmically to the left and right side of the trail. Your task is to ride in the direction your friend indicates. As she moves her arms to point in a different direction, you must steer your board in that direction. Remind your friend that it's bad form to steer you smack into a tree, or a nearby skier.

Practice these drills until you can rhythmically connect turns of different sizes. Start with long turns, and, as you develop proficiency, gradually make them quicker and shorter. You'll need to intensify your steering movements, and adjust the timing of your edge change and flexing and extending movements accordingly. It's important to be able to make shorter turns if you want to ride narrower, steeper trails.

Rhythm Changes

After you can make turns rhythmically down the slope, try changing the rhythm. This will develop your ability to turn intentionally, not by accident. Once again, counting, envisioning corridors, and using a changing musical beat are all useful ways to develop rhythm — and to change it.

USE A COUNT Try four short turns, then two long ones, back to four short ones, and so on.

RIDE THE TORNADO Connect turns to produce the shape of a funnel. Start by making long turns using the entire width of the slope. Make subsequent turns increasingly quicker and closer together. For a good cue, use a count. Start with a four count for the toe- and heel-side turns, then make the next two turns on a three count, the next two on a two count, and so forth. At the end of each turn series, stop and admire your handiwork. Use the track as a critique to see if your heel-side turn is as round as your toe-side turn and vice versa. Strive for symmetry.

INVERT IT After making tornado turns, try scribing an inverted tornado. Start with short counts on the first turns, and progress to higher counts on subsequent turns. Check your tracks to gauge your effectiveness.

CHANGE LANES Imagine the trail as being divided into two lanes of equal width. Start by making rhythmic short turns down the right lane. After making a series of four or five turns, make a longer turn to "change lanes" into the left lane, and make the same number of turns as you did in the right lane before making a longer turn back into the right lane. After you can change lanes consistently, try splitting the trail into three, then four lanes. As you transition from one lane to the next, make a long, round turn, rather than a straight traverse.

ADJUSTING TURNS TO TERRAIN

On a snowboard, it's crucial to look ahead and plan for steeper or flatter sections of trail. You want to anticipate terrain changes that will result in speed changes. It's heartbreaking to run out of speed on a flat section of trail. You then have to unclip your rear binding and limp across to where the hill begins again. Plan ahead! Where it's steep,

TORNADO TURNS Smoothly transition from making large to small turns so that your track resembles a tornado when viewed from its side. This develops your ability to precisely regulate the shape of your turns.

LANE CHANGES Wouldn't the slopes be the perfect location for a spanking-new super highway? That's just what you'll create (mentally, at least) as you envision parallel lanes stretching down the hill. Make your turns within a single lane (as you did in corridor turns) and then smoothly change lanes to an adjoining one. Rather than simply traversing straight between lanes, try to shape a smooth, round arc – a big turn – as you make the change. Go back and forth between lanes, just as you do when you're passing the slow drivers on your way to the slopes on a big powder day!

ADJUSTING TURN SHAPE FOR CHANGES IN TERRAIN Look ahead and plan your turns according to upcoming terrain changes. As you change from steep to flat terrain you'll need to adjust the shape of your turn. Make turns that finish across the fall line whenever you want to slow down (steeper slopes). As you transition from steep to flat terrain, allow your board to point more down the hill through the turn's finish. This will allow you to carry speed and avoid infuriatingly long skating expeditions across flat sections.

WET-BUTT SYNDROME Until you learn to build a platform so that you can fasten your rear foot while standing up (see page 73), you'll have to sit down and live with a wet butt.

make broader turns across the fall line to control your speed. To help carry speed across flats or down gentler slopes, steer your turns more directly down the fall line before you reach the terrain change.

Quick Stops

If there are gentle, uncrowded slopes on the way from the steeper practice area back to the lift, try riding your board straight down the hill to a quick stop on either edge (please do not try this on a crowded slope or in designated slow areas). Increase your speed by spending more time following the fall line. Remember, on steeper terrain you'll enjoy dramatic acceleration through the middle of each turn, and it's important that you become comfortable with speed before you start turning on steep inclines. That comfort comes from knowing that you can reliably slow down or stop when you're going fast.

Practice the following for more experience:
● Make a quick stop on a relatively steep, groomed slope. Bend your legs as you come to a stop and see if you can remain in balance for a moment after you do.
● After mastering the quick stop toe side and heel side, connect a series of them. Smoothly extend your legs and rapidly steer your board across the hill to a quick stop on your new edge. Flex your legs as you stop in balance.
● When you can connect a series of quick stops in balance, try doing so while maintaining a constant speed. See how slowly you can go as you link quick stops. Challenge your friends to a Slow Race, in which the boarder who goes down the slope the slowest (while remaining moving) wins.

AVOID SLAMS ON THE FLATS

The problem You're able to connect turns down beginner trails and are starting to explore other green-circle terrain. You come across a situation where you need to cross a long, flat section of trail. Don't make the mistake of pointing your board straight down the fall line and riding it flat to carry speed on this section, or you'll risk a high-speed, edge-catching wipeout. You'll also suffer the indignity of having to unclip your rear foot and limp/skate the rest of the way across the flat.

The solution On long, flat sections of trail, keep your board tilted on the uphill edge and make really loooong turns, with your angle of attack mostly down the fall line. The longer turns help you to maintain speed, and by remaining on your edges, you avoid the slam.

- Challenge yourself by exploring how many turns you can make on a particular slope (and then try to beat your record).

Flat-Ground 360-Degree Spins

These simple spins start you down the long, slippery slope to being a freestyle junkie. They also work to develop turning power, edge awareness, and balance. Plus, they're fun! Here's how to start spinning your first day out:

1. From a toe-side traverse, carry a little speed and steer the tip of your board *up* the hill.

2. Continue steering it so that the tip points directly up the hill.

3. Once your board points straight up the hill, shift weight to your downhill (rear) foot. Smoothly change to your heel edge.

4. Continue steering the tip of the board through the spin by pushing downhill with the front foot. Look in the direction you are spinning and stay balanced over the board (no leaning to the side).

5. Stop steering when your board is across the fall line on the heel edge.

6. Practice until you can consistently spin 360s starting from your toe edge.

7. Reverse the process to spin heel side.

Quality Mileage

Now that you're able to connect turns and adjust their shape for the terrain you're on, it's

TAKE A STAND ON WET BUTTS

Most experienced riders choose to fasten their rear foot into the binding while standing. It's faster, safer, uses less energy, and most important, helps you to avoid the dreaded wet-butt syndrome. But to do so, you need to learn how to build a platform on which to perch as you fasten your binding. Here's how:

1. Start by facing downhill with the board across the hill and your weight on your free foot, which should be uphill from your snowboard.

2. Keep the board tilted on its heel edge.

3. Keeping your weight on your free foot, use the board to construct a small, flat platform on which to stand. A quick chopping motion works best on groomed surfaces, and a gentler scraping and tapping fills the bill in loose snow or powder. Your flat platform, when finished, should be at least the length and width of your board, and should be exactly across the hill.

4. Test the platform by placing your snowboard on it and balancing – if you don't slide and can balance on the board, stop building.

Use the platform to balance on your board while fastening your rear foot into the binding. Remember that all other rules for fastening your bindings still apply – ensuring that no snow is lodged between the boot and the binding, that your foot is positioned all the way to the rear of the binding, and that the binding is fastened securely.

Building a platform is useful *any* time you stop on a slope and want to remain standing. One of the hardest things to do is balance on a board on a slope when you're not moving, which is why you often see other riders sprawled on the snow like human flotsam. You can astonish your friends with your balancing powers by building a secret platform under you each time you stop to wait for them. As you are stopping, use a small hopping motion to create the platform.

time to take your turns on a grand safari of the mountain's green-circle (beginner) trails. Continue to practice, varying the shape, size, and rhythm of your turns. This will refine your ability to make key movements, and to quickly become a more versatile snowboarder.

As your skills develop, move up to groomed blue-square (intermediate) trails. When you encounter steeper slopes, don't forget the usefulness of sideslips, traverses, reverses, and garlands if the terrain or snow conditions feel too challenging. Use them when you need to, and practice connecting turns whenever you can. Go snowboarding as often as you can. This enviable assignment is the best way to improve on your board.

THE CODE (AND ITS TRANSLATION)

A snow-covered mountain can be enjoyed in many ways. At Alpine resorts, you may see people using snowboards, Alpine or Telemark skis, or snowshoes. Regardless of how you decide to enjoy the slopes, it's vitally important that you show courtesy and respect to others. Be aware that there are elements of risk in snowboarding that common sense can help reduce. Observe the following code and share with other people the responsibility for a great experience on the slopes.

Ride in control and so that you can stop or avoid other people or objects. Choose terrain and speeds appropriate for your ability level. Don't get in over your head. If you are a beginner, don't go up the lift until you are sure you can get on and off, and can handle the terrain it serves. If you are more experienced, don't let your friends talk you into a double-diamond bump run, jumping off a cliff, or venturing into the trees until you are confident that you can handle the situation in total control.

People ahead of you have the right of way. It is your responsibility to avoid them. Anticipate the unexpected, such as someone ahead of you making a sudden turn or stopping. It is not acceptable to run over someone and self righteously claim "they cut me off." If you ride in control and allow people ahead of you the right of way, you'll be able to avoid them, even if they change directions unexpectedly. Observe posted slow zones and do not scare beginners by zooming by them at warp speed. If you want to go fast, do it on an advanced-level slope.

When starting downhill or merging onto a trail, look uphill and yield to others. When you are driving a car on the expressway, you don't want to pull out in front of a fast-moving semi. The same holds true for snowboarding. Wait your turn at the halfpipe and in the terrain park. If you're blasting carved arcs across a wide slope, check uphill before you turn; sometimes people don't anticipate how quickly you can slice across the slope (and into their path).

Prevent runaway equipment. Use a leash, and carry your board with care.

Observe all posted signs and warnings. Keep off closed trails and out of closed areas. Reduce your speed in slow and family zones. Don't jump where it's prohibited. *Never* duck under a rope (no matter how good the powder looks on the other side). If a trail is closed, it's closed for a reason — your safety.

RidingPowder
your guide to powder mastery

RidingPowder
your guide to powder mastery

Fresh powder can enhance both the aesthetic pleasures of an Alpine environment and the sensations of riding. After a storm, new-fallen snow highlights surrounding peaks and clings to tree branches, sparkling irresistibly in the early morning sunshine. You might be tempt-ed to simply stand and gawk at the beauty surrounding you, but don't. Snowboarding in fresh, untracked powder can be one of life's greatest experiences. That is, if you know how to ride in it.

Notice that I said "in." Snowboarding in powder is a three-dimensional experience. You ride *in* the snow, not on it as you do over groomed trails. The added resistance that comes from your board riding through the snow rather than over it means you must adjust your key movements. If you make the adjustments, you'll enjoy boarding in fresh powder more than in any other snow (and will probably start thinking seriously about booking that heli-boarding vacation to New Zealand this summer). If you don't make the adjustments, you'll end up tired, wet, cold, and frustrated. You decide.

PREREQUISITES To get the most from your first-ever powder experience, you must be able to link short turns down groomed intermediate trails. You also need fresh powder (see "Finding Powder," page 79). The more, the better (as you'll soon find out).

TERRAIN Find an uncrowded, reasonably steep green (beginner) or easy blue (intermediate) trail. You're looking for sections of smooth, untracked snow (tracked-up sections are adequate, but you'll suffer heaps of turbulence as you ride over the tracks). It's best if you can find a trail that has been partially groomed, so that you can move from groomed snow to deep powder as you develop your skills.

THE ROAD TO POWDER MASTERY

On an untracked, gentle slope with a good runout, practice going straight down the hill through the powder. One key to riding powder is to go fast. This allows your board to plane closer to the surface of the snow, where you can more easily steer. It's similar to waterskiing, in which getting up is one of the hardest parts: Once you are planing on the water's surface, it's easy to turn.

Your board's width will help you to float through the powder. If you are an Alpine skier, you'll delight in the extra flotation provided by a snowboard — it's far easier to board in deep powder than to ski. As you develop confidence, ride down steeper slopes, but make sure that you have plenty of space and a good runout as you practice.

Next, add gentle bouncing movements to your straight run, as if you are bouncing on a trampoline but trying not to catch air. This will make your board "porpoise" alternately deeper and shallower in the snow, an important technique to know for turning in powder. Porpoising is also an excellent way to assess the snow's characteristics. Ultralight powder rides differently than fresh, slightly wet powder (see "Handling Heavy, Wet Glop," page 83). If you are practicing on somewhat steeper

GENTLY BOUNCE TO GET YOUR BOARD TO THE SNOW'S SURFACE Bouncing will get your board to porpoise through the deep stuff. This rider's board is coming out of the snow, which will allow him to easily turn it. Time your turn so that it happens at the top of the bounce and you'll soon find yourself a powder virtuoso.

POWDER CHAMPS

Many ski areas hold Powder 8 competitions for snowboarders and Alpine skiers. Host areas close a section of the mountain prior to the competition, assuring competitors of an untracked powder slope on which to perform. A panel of judges evaluates competitors' synchronized powder eights. Scores are based on each two-person team's synchronization, symmetry, and roundness of turns. The best regional competitors win cash and prizes, and qualify for the Grand National Powder 8 Championships, held annually at Jackson Hole, Wyoming. National champions compete in the World Powder 8 Championships, hosted by Mike Wiegle Heli-Skiing in British Columbia, Canada.

POWDER CARVING Hard boots and carving boards are not just for groomed cruisers. Being narrow, they may not float as well as fat freeriding boards, but hey, this will just make the powder seem deeper!

slopes, bounce during toe- and heel-side traverses if you are not completely comfortable doing it while going straight down the hill.

Pay attention to the amount of springiness in the snow and the rebound that you can get when you bounce. As you gain confidence, try pulling your legs and feet up underneath you. Use the bounce and the active retraction of your legs to bring the board up to the surface of the snow. Try to get the board to bounce out of the snow completely. Then stop at the side of the trail and examine your tracks: You

CLEANSE YOUR LENS

Do not pull your goggles up onto your forehead if your head or hat is wet or snowy. The evaporating moisture from the melting snow on your hat and head conspire to turn the inside of your goggles into a terrarium. If it's snowing, or if you're riding in deep powder, it's best to always keep your goggles on. If they do get foggy, swab them gently with a dry tissue. You can find one at the base of most lifts — or bring a soft, dry swab or chammy cloth with you.

can see where the board rides higher and lower in the snow.

Turn Off the Rebound

Now learn to use this rebound to turn in powder. As always, timing is key. It's easiest to start your turns when the board is near the surface of the snow, so time the initiation of the turn near the top of your bounce. Start by making your turns mostly down the fall line: bounce, turn, bounce, turn. As you move to steeper terrain, progress to steering the board across the hill at sharper angles. Once you master the timing of bouncing and turning, and get into a rhythm, you'll find yourself effortlessly linking turns to the bottom of the slope.

You may need to intensify the energy you put into your steering movements to steer your board across the hill in deep snow. If you find yourself having trouble, practice pushing the tail of your board aggressively through the middle to the end of your turns on groomed snow. This will help you to develop the strong turning power necessary to

INTENSIFY THE ENERGY you put into your steering movements to steer across the hill in deep powder.

FINDING POWDER

Because deep, untracked powder never lasts long, one of your greatest challenges is simply finding it. To do so, get out early, before all of the late risers, who will soon run rampant over your pristine practice area. If you are first on the chairlift line on a powder day, you are guaranteed freshies (first tracks) for at least the first run. That means be at the loading area *before* the lift opens. As you wait for the lift to open, you'll enjoy the energy of the folks crazy enough to be there with you — these are hard-core riders and skiers, people for whom powder is all-important.

As the popular trails get tracked, look for lesser-used, out-of-the-way trails for more untracked snow. Ski patrollers, instructors, or locals will point the way, but don't expect locals to reveal to you their favorite powder stashes. These are some of skiing's and boarding's most closely guarded secrets and if they tell you, they probably will have to kill you.

Finally, look for small untracked powder stashes on the sides of trails. If you plan wisely, you can enjoy fresh powder while others are struggling with chopped-up snow.

Keep Your Board Afloat

People often plunge over the tip of the board when riding in deep powder. If you put too much weight on your front foot, you'll sink the tip and crash (a phenomenon known among surfers as "pearling"). Weight your rear foot when you ride in deep powder to keep your board floating.

If you expect to ride in deep powder all day, remount your bindings (assuming your board has inserts) so that they are farther back on the board. It's a simple procedure: All you need to do is remove the mounting screws and remount the bindings using inserts farther back on the board. Moving both the front and the rear binding 1 inch back will help you to float your tip in powder and avoid pearling.

Getting Up

If you happen to fall in deep powder, you may find it difficult to get up again. Loose snow compacts as you push against it, and you'll find yourself pushing your arm, elbow, (or shoulder — lucky you!) deep in the fresh stuff as you try to stand up.

If you do go down, stand up on the toe side — it's much easier to get up from a kneeling position. If you find yourself sitting in the snow, roll over onto your knees and the toe side. If all else fails, you can unclip your rear binding and use your free foot to help you get back up.

As you stand, try to keep your board near the snow surface. If your board is buried, dig it out (if you can, without removing your boots from the bindings). It's nearly impossible to get moving on a deeply buried snowboard. Get up fast — your friends will not likely wait for you if there is untracked snow nearby.

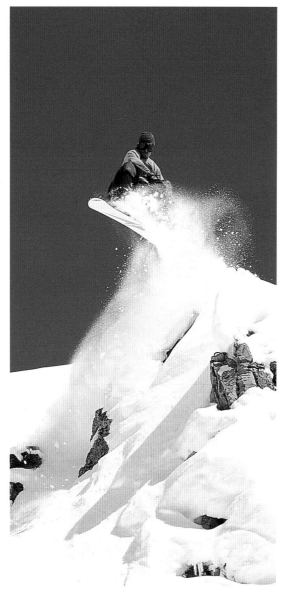

SOFT LANDING Before trying to get big air in powder, always check out the landing zone to make sure your re-entry will be soft. Powder can cover dangerous rocks.

steer the board in deep snow.

If you're with a friend, try riding figure eights down the hill, switching leads. Mirroring another's track is a fun, and beneficial, snowboarding drill.

FINDING POWDER Rise early and get up the lift first to find fresh, untracked powder like this.

CONTROLLING SPEED IN DEEP POWDER

If you happen to turn across the slope to slow down immediately before or on a long flat area, be prepared for an exhausting posthole/ swim through the deep snow. Avoid that fate by looking ahead to read the terrain, so that you can plan your route and moves in order to carry speed across the flats in powder. As you approach a flat section, maintain speed by keeping the tip of your board pointed mostly down the hill as you turn.

Ride Tracks across Flats

If, despite your best efforts to maintain speed, you find yourself slowing down, try to ride in someone's track. This lessens the resistance of traveling through deep snow and allows you to maintain more speed. If you are with a group, leapfrog across flat areas, with the lead person breaking trail, and subsequent riders using that person's track to scoot farther along the trail.

Use Powder to Slow Down

There are times, on the other hand, when you'll be glad to use powder to slow down. When you're riding a narrow, rutted, tracked section (such as on narrow catwalks or when you ride through the trees), and you feel the need to slow down, ride into a section of deep powder and turn. The extra resistance provided by the powder will slow you down quickly.

FINDING MORE POWDER You can often find freshies on the sides of the trails (and in the trees) long after the middle of the slopes are all tracked out.

neath you. Remember: Use tracks to carry speed; use deep snow to slow down. In either case, anticipate a sudden change in speed and position your weight accordingly.

HANDLING CHOPPED-UP POWDER

If, for some ridiculous reason, you decide to sleep in on a powder day and don't get on the slopes until midmorning, chances are good you will encounter chopped-up powder. This once-smooth snow, now cut by the countless tracks of your powder-crazed predecessors, is more challenging to ride than the untracked variety. Expect sudden changes in speed and direction as your board runs through tracks and snow piles pushed up by other riders and skiers. Here are some tips for handling the choppy stuff:

● Look for untracked areas between the tracks. It's easier to make your turns in smooth snow.

● When riding across choppy areas, drop your hips closer to the snow. Lowering your center of weight enhances stability in turbulent snow.

● As the snow continues to get tracked out, it will get pushed into small (and not so small) piles. Anticipate a sudden deceleration as you ride into a pile, and push your board out ahead of you just before impact. As you run into the pile, relax your legs. The snow's additional resistance will push your feet back underneath you, keeping you ready, and in balance for the next one.

Get Back!

When riding, get your weight back during a transition from groomed to deep powder snow. If you don't, the sudden deceleration might throw you over the tip of your board. Drop your hips and push your feet forward into the deep snow. At the moment of contact, relax your legs slightly to absorb the impact. The sudden extra resistance that occurs when you hit the deep snow will push your feet back under your body.

Similarly, get your weight forward when you ride from deep powder to groomed snow. You don't want your board, as it hits the groomed snow, to accelerate out from under-

GAITER AIDS

In deep powder, gaiters are very helpful, especially around your ankles, wrists, and waist. Do whatever you can to keep loose snow from penetrating your outer layer: An avalanche *inside* your clothes is hard to bear — and is entirely avoidable.

HANDLING CHOPPED-UP POWDER Drop your hips closer to the snow to lower your center of gravity while riding over tracked powder.

HANDLING HEAVY, WET GLOP

Cheerfully called "Sierra Cement" or "Cascade Concrete" after the mountain ranges where it is prevalent, ultraheavy, water-saturated snow can be anything but cheerful to ride. Here are some tips for coping with concrete:

GO FAST Don't complete your turns as much as you would in other circumstances. You need to maintain your momentum to make it across any flat areas. This is crucial, because skating/wallowing through such wet snow on a board is not fun, especially when your

A STICKY POWDER PROBLEM

The problem It's a powder day. You grab your board and run outside, fasten the bindings, and try to skate to the lifts for first tracks. Your board, however, has other ideas: It refuses to move, sticking like it was super-glued to the snow. You disconsolately watch your "friends" as they glide to the lift and head up for freshies, leaving you behind to fend off the mysterious force that has taken over your board.

What's really happening Your board is warm, and the fresh, loose powder snow melts instantly when it touches the warm base. It then attracts all of its flaky friends, which adhere to the moist snow and form a "snowberg" on the bottom of your board, large enough to sink the Titanic.

The solution Scrape the accumulated snow and ice off your board with a flat *plastic* scraper (one made of steel, iron, or concrete may damage the base). In a pinch, a car windshield ice scraper, cassette case, or even a credit card has been known to work. Resolve to let your board cool off to snow temperature before you lay it base down on the snow. Just placing the board in the rack while you purchase your lift ticket will do the trick.

skating foot sinks down 3 feet with every push!

GET LOW Anticipate the sudden deceleration that accompanies riding into heavy, wet snow; its resistance can instantly stop your board, throwing you (if unprepared) over the tip for a classic "endo" or face plant.

GET BACK Be ready to instantly shift your weight back (by pushing your feet and board forward) when you begin to feel your board slowing down.

READ THE SNOW You'll go faster in snow that's already been tracked. Fresh, wet, slushy snow provides tremendous resistance, slowing your board down and making turning harder. Go straight, gathering enough speed to plane your board near the snow surface, before you try to turn. Let your board run and use your momentum to make long turns.

LOOK FOR UNTRACKED AREAS The turbulence caused by crossing existing tracks can throw you off balance. If everything is tracked out, try to turn between the tracks; you'll find it easier.

RIDE WITH THE SUN In the Northern Hemisphere most ski areas face north and east: Less sun means that they'll be able to hold snow a bit longer. Exposure to direct sunlight first softens snow, then turns it wet and sloppy. In general, that means that the left side of the trail will receive early-morning sunlight first, with the middle and right side getting more direct sunlight toward the end of the day.

BE ALERT TO THE SUN'S ACTION ON THE SNOW By strategically riding sun-softened snow before it turns to slush, you'll enjoy the best conditions that a trail has to offer. Ride the sun-warmed sections in the early morning, then look for shady areas during the mid- to late afternoon. You'll find harder snow in these areas and be better able to glide (rather than skate) all the way to the bottom.

AVOID DIRTY SNOW The pine tar, pollen, and other debris from trees and the grease emitted from the snowmaking and grooming machinery will foul your board's base, causing it to drag. Keep your base clean. Most rental-shop or ski-school personnel are happy to help by providing base-cleaning solvent. There are now simple citrus solvents that quickly cut through that dark filmy layer, allowing you to once again glide better on wet, heavy snow (see Chapter 12 for more information on prepping your base).

BEWARE OF YOUR BOARD GETTING BURIED IN HEAVY, WET SNOW If, for any reason, you need to stop and your board bogs down under the snow, it's helpful to bend over and push the snow off with your hands. The weight of the snow will make getting started again difficult, and will make it much harder to turn your board.

SAFETY ISSUES
What You Can't See
Can Hurt You

Deep powder can conceal objects or obstacles on a slope, including buried rocks, stumps, and holes. Hitting a buried object can ruin your board — or your day. Keep in mind that new snow can also obscure challenging terrain (such as ice) just underneath. The snow may be deep enough to cover these ice bumps, but not deep enough to float you over them (this is sometimes called "dust on crust"). Because you can't see them, you often end up getting thrown by them. Therefore, always be alert in these

conditions for frozen bumps or objects underneath the fluff.

Be Alert for Avalanche Risk

I am assuming that you're riding within a ski area's boundaries and, after a powder storm, that avalanche-control work has taken place. Even so, despite the best efforts of area avalanche-control personnel, there may exist some areas within bounds that slide. The key is to be careful in deep snow (see pages 142 – 146).

● Tree wells can kill you. Over the years, several people have lost their lives falling into tree wells formed around the trunks of evergreens. In deep snow, be *extremely* careful around the trunks of evergreens, keeping a distance of at least 12 feet.

● Be careful riding in steep gullies or drainages, called sloughs. As you ride down, snow on the sides can slide down and bury you.

● Even though that powder stash below the rope may look tempting, keep out! The ski patrol closes trails for a reason (your safety). Avalanches can kill you. Always obey posted trail closings.

SmoothingOut theBumps
tips for tackling the most turbulent terrain

6

SmoothingOut theBumps

tips for tackling the most turbulent terrain

As you develop proficiency on a board and progress to steeper trails, you'll encounter bumps. Bumps, or moguls, occur wherever a slope is steep and not regularly groomed. Turning skis or a board on a steep slope displaces snow, pushing it downhill through the end of each turn. As this snow accumulates, it forms small piles. Multiply this by a few gazillion riders and skiers and you have many piles of snow, which influence the path of descent of all subsequent users. The configuration of any bump trail, then, reflects the overall riding ability of those who preceded you. Irregularly spaced, choppy bumps are formed by less-skilled riders and skiers (and are, perversely, harder to ride). You'll usually find the most agreeable, round, rhythmic bumps on slopes used only by the most expert of riders and skiers. Quite the paradox.

Things can come at you fast in the bumps. Quickness and balance are crucial to mastering moguls. Bump riding demands that you be able to perform key movements in a dynamic, ever-changing environment. You need to be able to make lightning-fast edging movements to respond to a varying fall line; quickly bend and extend your legs to absorb each bump as you ride over it; make rapid fore and aft adjustments to balance through your board's decelerations and accelerations as you climb and descend each bump; and make quick, powerful steering movements as you navigate a path over, around, and through the bumps. All at the same time! Bump riding puts your ability to make key movements to the test, and challenges even

ABSORBING A BUMP Using your legs like shock absorbers to smooth your ride is crucial to success in the bumps. In this sequence, the rider looks ahead as she approaches the bump (1). She has pushed her feet forward to anticipate the slight deceleration that will occur when her board hits the bump. As she hits the bump, the rider relaxes her legs, allowing her feet to be pushed back underneath her (2). At the same time, she bends deeply with her legs so that the bump does not throw her skyward. Note how she keeps her hands forward (within her field of vision) and keeps looking ahead. As she rides down the back side of the bump (3), she extends her bent legs, allowing her to be ready to absorb the next bump.

the most skilled riders. So, make sure that you're ready, and then go for it!

PREREQUISITES Before you venture into the bumps, you should be able to link short turns with speed and control on steep intermediate and easy expert groomed trails. If you can't make turns small enough to navigate around tightly spaced moguls, you'll be at their mercy, rather than in control. Your two major challenges in the bumps are controlling your speed, and smoothing out a sometimes incredibly bumpy ride.

TERRAIN Look for a wide intermediate trail with small, well-spaced bumps and progress to steeper, narrower trails (and bigger bumps) as you develop control and confidence. A trail that is half-bumped and half-groomed is the best place to start. The groomed area (called the "chicken lane") offers an escape route should you get in over your head. Ask a ski patroller or instructor for information on the best trail to start riding the bumps.

FIRST BUMP RUN

Focus on absorbing each bump. Your legs need to work like shock absorbers to smooth your ride in moguls. Ideally, riding over the bumps should not move your upper body up and down: Your legs should bend or extend to absorb each bump as you ride over it.

Start by traversing *slowly* across the slope and focus on absorbing each bump as you ride over it. Keep your legs half-bent, so that you have an equal range of movement for both bending and extending. If you ride with straight legs, you'll be unable to lengthen them if your board drops into a trough; if you ride fully crouched, you'll have no where to go to absorb a bump as you ride over it.

1. As your board hits a bump, relax your legs and allow the bump to push your feet up underneath you. Bend your ankles, knees, and hips. You may also have to bend at the waist and with your back to absorb extra-big bumps. Try pulling your knees toward your chest as

Beginning riders often bend their legs to absorb the upward slope of the first bump they pass over, and then keep them bent as they go down the back side of the bump. When they hit the next bump, they can't bend their legs to absorb it, because they are *already* bent. The bump sends them flying. Remember to push down with your feet on the back side of a bump (extend your legs); you'll be ready to bend your legs to absorb the next bump.

you go over the really big ones.

2. As you crest the top of the bump and descend its back side, extend your legs. Keep your board in contact with the snow.

3. Practice until you can traverse the slope and absorb each bump, in balance, on both the toe edge and heel edge.

4. Progressively increase your speed by traversing closer to the fall line as you develop the ability to absorb bumps.

Developing Fore and Aft Balance

To complicate matters, your board changes speed as it climbs and descends bumps, slowing as it climbs a bump and accelerating as it goes down its back side. Your absorption move has to be coordinated with a subtle push or pull with your feet to anticipate these speed

changes. Push your feet slightly forward immediately before hitting the bump and allow the impact and deceleration of the board to push them back underneath you. As you crest the bump, keep your weight forward (pull your feet back) by extending your hips toward the tip of the board as you start down its back side to anticipate the board accelerating.

Charting Your Course

At first, navigating through the bumps may seem far more challenging than riding on a groomed trail. To successfully take them on, you need to look several bumps ahead to plan your route. The path, or line, you take through the bumps directly influences the speed and difficulty of your descent. Your choices are riding over the tops of the bumps, through the troughs between the bumps, or somewhere in between.

Riding over the tops of the bumps can help you to unweight — and turn — your board, and will fully tax your absorption skills. Riding the troughs between the bumps provides a smooth, fast path, but can be very difficult if the troughs are icy, narrow slots. Riding the sides of the bumps is sometimes the smoothest path. Look for loose, shaved snow if there are icy patches between the bumps and make your turns there. Usually, a ride through moguls will include all three routes, so it's a good idea to practice each one separately. Start with traverses and work your

THE GREAT TERRAIN COMBO PLATTER

You'll find a wide variety of slope profiles on a single bump trail. The front side to the top of each bump is least steep; think of it as green-circle terrain. Make your first turns there. The sides and back side of each bump can provide blue- and black-diamond challenges, respectively. As you develop your skills, progress to making your turns there.

way into the fall line as you gain confidence.

TURNING ON BUMPS

First try turning at the top of a bump. You can use the bumps to your advantage by turning on top of the bump, or bouncing off the side of the bump and using it to redirect your board. The bump will help to unweight your board and will provide the least amount of resistance to your turning movements.

1. Look ahead and choose the bump on which you want to turn.

2. As you hit the bump, gently *extend* your legs as you run up and over the bump. This will help you to unweight and turn the board. This is the opposite of the movement that you use to absorb the bumps. Remember, flex to absorb bumps, gently extend to start a turn.

3. Make a quick turn at the top of the bump. Control your speed by steering your board completely across the fall line. Because the tip and tail are not in contact with the snow, it's easiest to steer the board here. Make a gentle extending movement that assists the bump in unweighting the board — and makes it easier to steer.

4. Keep your weight forward and the tip of

TURN ON THE TOP OF THE BUMP As I approach the bump on my heel edge, I push my feet forward, anticipating a slight deceleration as my board strikes – and climbs – the bump **(1)**. At the top of the bump **(2)**, I make the turn and smoothly change to the toe edge. Note how the tip of the board stays in contact with the snow as it starts down the bump's back side (you need to move forward, toward the tip of the board to do this). I bend my legs slightly through the turn's finish **(3)**, which allows me to further bend them if I need to absorb the next bump – or to extend them to unweight the board again. I control my speed by using my legs to steer the board across the fall line **(4)** under a stabilized upper body – which is now facing in the direction of my next turn. I can then uncoil my twisted midbody to help start my next turn.

the board *on the snow* as you crest the bump and descend its back side.

5. Anticipate a slight acceleration as your board glides down the steeper back side of the mogul.

8. As you become better at absorbing bumps, turning on them, and controlling your speed, turn more often and increase your angle of attack.

Steer with your lower body. You need to use the powerful steering movements of your legs to hold the board on course and prevent it from ricocheting off the side of a bump in an unexpected direction. Keep your upper body and hands quiet *and oriented down the hill*. Freestylers who ride 0-degree stances will not face directly down the slope, but will find their upper body facing the direction of their upcoming turn as they steer their board across the hill underneath them. Riders who use more angled stances will find themselves facing farther down the fall line. With either type of stance, as you steer the board across the hill, you'll create a twisted relationship between your upper and lower body, which you can then unwind to start your next turn.

Use the Tip Turn for Steep Bumps

After you master riding easy blue bumps, you'll undoubtedly want to progress to steeper slopes and more challenging bumps. Here's how to take on steeper bumps (or any steep slope). Instead of pushing and pulling your feet in opposition to each other to steer the board around a point between your bindings, move both feet *in the same direction* to swing the tail of the board across the hill. The board should pivot around a point near its tip. The

STEEP BUMPS Beginners often wildly swing their arms and torso while riding steep bumps. To avoid this, focus on keeping your hands still and in front of you.

6. Ride down the back of the bump on your new edge.

7. Traverse the slope again, focusing on absorbing each bump you ride over, and make another turn on top of a bump on the far side of the slope.

RIDE THE CONTOUR LINE

As you ride down a bump field, envision a topographic map with contour lines demarcating different elevations in the bumps. Try to ride along a single contour line, connecting the bumps without gaining or losing altitude.

THE TIP TURN will help you to get down steep slopes (including steep bumps). As you finish a turn on one edge (1), gently hop and pivot a turn off the tip of your board (2). You should hop so that the tail of your board literally comes off the snow, making it easier to swing it through a turn. Finish your turn by bending your legs (3), which sets you up again to hop – and tip turn – to your new edge (4,5). Make a tip turn off the top of the bump on steep bump trails. It'll help to keep your weight forward and your speed in control.

board with the tip still on the snow, try swinging the tail of the board to either side while it is unweighted.

4. Initiate your jump off of your toe or heel edge, moving both feet *away from* the direction of your intended turn. If you keep the tip on the snow, it will not move as you do this, but the tail of the board will.

5. Practice until you can consistently do tip turns in either direction on flat ground.

6. Take your tip turns to a groomed trail and practice them while in motion. Jump from one edge to the other, swinging the tail of the board around and pivoting off the nose of the board.

tip turn enhances your ability to balance and control your speed on mogul fields — especially steep ones. Here's how to do it:

1. On flat ground, with both feet fastened into your bindings, try jumping up with both feet, keeping your tip on the snow.

2. See if you can balance briefly on the tip.

3. As you develop the ability to unweight your

You can use the tip turn to great advantage in the bumps and on steep terrain. It helps to keep your weight forward as your board accelerates down the back side of a bump, and allows you to maintain contact with the snow, giving you much greater control.

EXTRA BUMP CHALLENGES

Try these fun and exciting maneuvers to continue to develop your skills in the bumps:

GIANT SLALOM TURNS IN THE BUMPS After perfecting short-radius turns in the bumps, try making longer turns. You'll need to bend and extend your legs to absorb several bumps through each turn. Practice until you can carve equally well on both the toe and heel edge.

DOUBLE-JUMPING THE BUMPS Sometimes it's easier to leap the gap between two bumps rather than ride through the trough separating them. Gauge your speed and spring at the top of the bump so that you land *on the back side* of the second bump. Bend your legs as you land. Practice on gentle bumps and progress to steeper ones as you develop your double-jumping skills.

360-DEGREE BUMP SPINS Try an on-the-snow spin off the top or side of a bump. Practice toe side and heel side.

FAKIE TURNS When you're feeling confident on bumps, try riding fakie. First start out traversing; then progress to turns as you develop your skills.

High-Performance Carving

getting the most from the design of your board

7

High-Performance Carving

getting the most from the design of your board

Carved turns, as opposed to skidded turns, open up a new level of riding excitement and challenge. Carving lets you unlock the awesome potential in your snowboard, enabling you to power across ice, through bumps, and down steeps. Being able to move so far into a

turn that your hips graze the snow, and carry that energy into the next turn is one of the most exciting things you'll ever do on snow.

PREREQUISITES Before learning to carve you should be comfortable linking skidded turns on blue-square (intermediate) trails.

TERRAIN Find a wide, uncrowded, groomed green-circle (easy) trail. It's best to learn to carve where it's relatively flat and then progress to steeper slopes.

SKIDDING vs. CARVING It's important to master skidding and stopping on your board *before* learning to carve. When skidding, you are moving the board both sideways and forward, and you are steering both by edging the board and twisting it around the pivot point between your feet. Skidded turns generate friction between the edge and the snow surface, helping you to slow down and stop. When carving, however, you are moving the board forward with no skidding. Turning is accomplished through edging alone, which means there will be some fairly extreme edging in your future. You need to steer the board so that the tip and tail pass through the same point in the snow. Because the board moves straight ahead, very little friction is generated between the edge and the snow. Therefore, to control speed you must adjust the *shape* of your turns. To slow down, you ride the turn across — and some-

USE THE SIDECUT TO CARVE ARCS When you can carve a traverse across the slope on either edge, explore using the sidecut to make a carved turn to a stop. Start by increasing your angle of attack (1) and steering the board so that the tip and tail pass through exactly the same point in the snow. You'll enjoy a bit more speed, which will allow you to bend your board more (it is the bent board that determines the shape of your carved arc). As your board bends (2), it will pull you through a round arc. Balance on your edge and let the sidecut do the work. Ride all the way across the hill to slow down (3). Check your track: if it's a razor-thin line you're doing it right!

times up — the hill. Until you are comfortable doing this, skid to slow down.

COUNTDOWN TO CARVING

5. Start, as you did with skidded turns, by trying to carve a traverse across the slope. Alternate between the toe and heel edge. Keep your weight centered between your feet. With their huge sidecuts, snowboards react quickly to weighting the tip or tail. For consistent carves, stay centered on the "sweet spot" between your bindings, with one edge or the other in contact with the snow at all times. Carving is pure forward movement. You'll know if you're doing it right by examining your track after each traverse. If you see a razor-thin line in the snow that looks like it was etched by a laser beam, you're carving. If you see a wider, smeared track,

you're skidding. Practice until you can slice across the slope on either edge.

4. As you gain confidence carving a traverse, point your board farther down the slope. You'll note that the board carves a curved track across the hill, eventually bringing you to a balanced stop. This is caused by the board's sidecut, which (when the board is decambered by your weight) causes it to turn. In other words, if you steer the board so that the tip and tail pass through the same point in the snow while it's on edge, the board will turn on its own. Eureka! Increase your angle of attack until you can point the board straight down the hill and carve an arc all the way across it on both the toe and heel edge.

3. As you traverse your way down the slope, explore adjusting the amount that you edge the board. Move your hips across the

ENGAGE THE DOWNHILL EDGE TO START YOUR CARVED TURN To ride the sidecut – and carve – through the entire turn you'll need to roll the board onto it's new edge at the top of the turn. Although moving to the downhill edge may seem suicidal at first (you'll catch your edge and slam if you are skidding), have faith. If you're carving, moving to your new edge will send you into some of your most exciting turns ever.

board toward the hill, and fine-tune with subtle movements of your knees, ankles, and feet to increase your edge angle. You'll find that tilting the board higher up on its edge makes it turn more sharply. Decreasing the amount of edge will make it turn more gradually. Practice until you are comfortable adjusting the amount of edging — and changing the shape of your arc — as you carve traverses across the hill.

2. On a relatively flat section of trail, practice smoothly rolling the board from the toe to the heel edge and back again as you go straight down the hill. Start by feeling the pull of the board's sidecut as you roll it on its edge and shape your carved turn across the hill. This smooth movement back and forth from edge to edge will help you exit one turn and enter the next.

1. Now for the fun part: As you carve a traverse across the slope, smoothly roll your board onto the *downhill* edge. This is a foreign concept for many boarders. Until now, engaging the downhill edge has caused a wipeout. The difference is that now your board is not moving sideways (skidding). When your board is moving straight ahead you *can* move to the downhill edge to start a turn. You'll find that the board magically pulls you into and through a magnificent carved turn. Stop and admire your track. It should be razor thin through the entire turn. Practice until you are comfortable rolling the board to either edge to start the turn.

As you gain ability, explore tilting the board higher to make a shorter-radius carve and a little lower to make a longer turn. Check your tracks often to ensure that you are slicing, not skidding. When you feel comfortable and can consistently carve turns on groomed green-circle slopes, practice on progressively steeper slopes. Remember, move straight ahead, engage the downhill edge, and get ready for the ride of your life!

CARVING AT HIGHER SPEEDS

Carving is faster than skidding because it causes so much less friction. That's why racers carve their turns. It's also why you'll need to develop speed control and the ability to manage G-forces when you carve. The following

RETRACTION TURNS Retraction turns allow you to better manage the forces generated by turning at higher speeds, and allow you to ride a greater variety of snow conditions and terrain. Extend your legs through the middle of your turn (1), then relax your legs and allow them to bend as you let your momentum carry you across the board to start your next turn (2). Extend again through the middle of your next turn (3) and repeat. When you make a retraction turn you should not lift your body any higher from the snow surface. You bend your legs as your board travels beneath you and extend your feet away from you through the middle of your next turn.

RETRACTION TURNS

A rising movement at the end of each turn is common among beginner and intermediate riders. While this motion is useful in many situations, you can also move the other way as you finish your turns. Retraction turns reverse the bending/extending sequence.

To understand the benefits of moving in this way, try the following exercise. Find a chair, step, or other slightly elevated platform, and explore two different ways to land as you step from this platform: first by trying to make as loud an impact as possible, then by trying to land as softly as possible. How do you move to create a thunderous landing? How is it different from a silent touchdown? And how can you apply this knowledge of how to work with forces while making turns on a snowboard?

When you turn a snowboard, redirecting your momentum creates force – particularly at the finish of a turn. If you are really zipping along and cut a hard turn, that force can be enormous. If you extend your legs as you did to create a loud landing, you'll only add to the forces present in that part of the turn. Sometimes the force you add is like the straw that broke the camel's back, causing your edge to blow out of the snow and sending you on an exciting but unintentional body slide. However, if you *flex* your legs through the end of a turn, you reduce the amount of force in that part of the turn, which can make the difference between crashing and continuing into the next turn.

When you make retraction turns, you *relax* your legs through the turn's finish, allowing them to bend as your momentum carries you across your board and into your new turn. As you guide your board through the middle of the turn, extend your feet out to the side, then flex again through the end of your turn (which starts the next one). Flexing through the finish of your turns will help to reduce pressure between your edge

CONTINUED ON NEXT PAGE

and the snow instead of adding to it. It's important to note that you extend your legs out to the side: this motion should not lift your body higher relative to the snow surface. Being able to perform retraction turns whenever forces get huge separates good riders from very good riders.

Retraction turns will allow you to make lightning-fast transitions from one turn to the next, and will enable you to more smoothly ride ice, bumps, powder, crud, and steeps – any situation where adding force at the end of the turn could blow you out of the snow. Practice these turns with a friend so that you can observe each other. Watch the hips and mid torso: this part of the body should not rise up at the end of the turn. When you can consistently perform retraction turns, work on adjusting the size of the turn. Go long, short, and in-between. Being able to make these turns will pump up your fun quotient by enhancing your versatility as a rider.

exercises will help you learn how to use your legs to work with the higher Gs.

Suspension System

PISTON TRAVERSE As you slice a traverse, rise and sink like a piston by extending and flexing your legs. Maintain an erect and stable upper body. See if you can rise and sink while slicing a clean arc across the slope. The trick is to make your extending and flexing movements without affecting the amount you edge the board. If these movements cause your edge angle to change, your board will either make a shorter or a longer turn. Try to maintain a consistent radius.

PISTON TURN When you can piston traverse a carved arc on either edge, make the same rising and sinking movements while connecting long, carved turns.

HOP TRAVERSES AND TURNS Now try gentle hops during traverses, then during long, carved turns. Practice until you can consistently hop and land in balance while carving turns.

Edge Control

To control the shape of a carved turn (and with it, your speed), you need to be able to adjust the amount that you edge your board. More edging will tighten the radius of your turn, decreasing your speed; less edging will make your turn run longer and closer to the fall line, increasing your speed. Where speed control is important, shape your turns so that you finish them with your board across the hill.

Here are two fun exercises used by racers and coaches to hone their ability to shape carved turns. Both use the unmistakable carved-turn track as a guide, so the very best time to do them is early in the morning, before crowds ski over your freshly groomed snow.

TOXIC WASTE TURNS Try to carve an arc uphill from your predecessor(s). If you touch or cross their track, you're "wasted." Increase the challenge by making progressively tighter arcs.

TOXIC WASTE TURNS You'll need a partner or a small group for this one. On one side of a wide, well-groomed, moderately pitched slope, have someone straight-run the slope for a short distance and then roll his board on its edge to carve across the hill to a stop. His track in the snow represents the edge of a toxic waste spill. The object is for you (and all subsequent riders) to follow the first person's track until you reach the point where he tilted the board high on its edge, and then to stay *above* his track as it comes across the hill by tilting your board higher on its edge. If you touch or go below the track ahead of you, you're wasted.

Alternate between toe and heel edge (or, if you're in a mixed group of goofy and regular riders, cutting alternate arcs to the left and right). Have people clear the practice area after their turn: You don't want to run someone over in your efforts to avoid the toxic waste area. Switch leaders so that everyone has the opportunity to lead and to follow. This develops the ability to use a high edge angle to cut a tight radius arc, and to manage the forces caused by turning so tightly.

RUNAWAY TRAIN Once again, you'll need a small group — four to six riders is best. Everyone needs to be able to link carved turns. Find a well-groomed, uncrowded, moderately sloped trail. You'll be descending the trail as a train: The lead rider is the locomotive, and the second rider is the coal car. Subsequent passenger, dining, and bar "cars" are followed by the caboose. Most trains stay on the same track, but not this one. The object, as you descend, is to carve a track 1 foot to the right of the track preceding yours. Keep a safe distance from the person ahead of you, and carve your path right next to hers. After a long series of turns, stop and give your predecessor feedback as to the accuracy of her riding (unless, of course, she was the leader). Was her track exactly 1 foot from the track preceding hers? Did she slice a clean arc the entire time? As you practice, swap roles so that everyone has a chance to lead and to follow. Then try riding 1 foot to the left of the track preceding yours.

If you select a trail under the lift, you'll be able to admire your handiwork — and get valuable feedback on your riding — on the way back up the hill. If you notice that you are able to complete the task toe side but not heel side (or vice versa), revise your training, and practice adjusting the shape of your carved arcs on that specific edge.

The point of the runaway train exercise is to force you to precisely adjust the shape of

On steeps, beginners often reach down toward the snow on the toe-side turn. This actually works to decrease the amount of edge angle between the board and the snow, and won't allow them to finish their turns as quickly. To avoid this, try lifting your rear arm up, and lower your hips toward the hill on your toe-side turn. Your shoulders should be parallel to the snow surface. This will help you to get maximum bite from your edge and enable you to carve extremely tight-radius turns toe side.

RUNAWAY TRAIN Your challenge is to carve a track exactly 1 foot to the right of the track preceding yours. Note that as you occupy positions farther back in the train the task becomes more challenging because you'll end up making a long turn in one direction and a short turn in the other.

You'll need to use the shape of your turn to slow down when you carve, sometimes extending your arc so that you actually start to travel uphill before starting your next turn. See how slow you can carve down the hill without losing the integrity of the arc.

your turns as you ride. The tighter the turn, the more you will need to tilt the board on its edge. As you occupy positions farther away from "the locomotive," you'll be forced to carve progressively longer and shorter turns on opposite edges.

In addition to edging precision, the runaway train exercise requires you to look several turns ahead. If you see that the locomotive has cut a hard turn across the trail, you'll need to be prepared to move accordingly before you get to that spot.

"Laying It Out"

On steep groomed terrain, long- to medium-radius carves are the most fun because of the degree that you need to move to the inside of the turn. This is where you see people really "laying it out," riding with their bodies brushing the snow. The delight of moving so far into a turn and standing against significant G-forces defies description. Here's how to try it:

1. As you finish a turn, relax your legs and allow your momentum to carry your body across the board into your next turn. Moving across the board engages your new edge at the top of the turn.

2. As with any carved turn, move to your new edge to start the turn.

3. Commit to the new turn. You have to let

yourself move downhill from your equipment, confident in your ability to guide it back underneath you by the time you get to the finish of the turn.

4. Create a high-edge angle early in the turn. The key to speed control on steeps is to shape a turn so that your board comes all the way across the hill through the turn's finish. Creating a high-edged angle early in the turn will help you quickly turn through — and across — the fall line. Try to tilt your board so high on its edge that it's perpendicular to the snow surface.

5. Flex deeply through the turn's finish. This allows you to effectively manage the G-forces created by turning.

6. Allow your decambered board's sidecut to bring you all the way across the hill before starting the next turn.

7. On extremely steep slopes you may need to allow your momentum to carry you *uphill* a bit. This will help to reduce speed before starting a new turn. On steeps, your carved track will resemble the interlocking pieces of a jigsaw puzzle.

8. Start the next turn by relaxing your legs through the turn's finish, and allowing your momentum to carry you down the hill to start a new turn.

HaveanIceDay

tips to master
ice and hard snow

8

HaveanIceDay

tips to master ice and hard snow

one. Most intermediate and advanced snowboarders have experienced hard, ultraslick snow and ice — and hate it. They can ride soft snow with ease, but when the snow turns hard and icy they lose their edge — and sometimes their patience. It's not surprising that many riders list ice as their least favorite surface.

Our experiences often reflect what we choose to focus on. If you regard ice as dreadful, it will be. But you can choose to view it as just another one of the challenges experienced when snowboarding. Riding ice requires sensitivity, subtlety, and precision in your movements, and provides *immediate* feedback if you are the least bit out of balance. In short, ice can be your ally in developing rock-solid snowboarding skills. Whether you perceive ice as friend or foe, learning the following tips will help you develop control and confidence on the slick stuff.

LESS IS MORE

Small movements get big results on this nearly friction-free surface. Big, abrupt movements will cause imbalance. The movements you use to balance on the board and to control your speed and direction must be smooth, accurate, and disciplined — or you will fall.

STAY CENTERED To control your speed and direction on a snowboard you need to balance over your edge. There is no room for error on ice. If you lean too far into the hill, or move

Despite all the advances in snowmaking and grooming that almost guarantee soft snow, you will still encounter ice and hard snow. Knowing how to handle it can make the difference between a fun, safe experience or a frustrating, unpleasant, or even dangerous

too far toward the tip or tail of the board, chances are you'll lose control or fall (or both). Balance by keeping your weight centered between your feet. *Do not* reach down toward the hill — especially on the toe side. This will bring your weight too far to the side of the board, reducing your effective edge angle (exactly the opposite of what you want to do to get your edge to grip).

EDGE FROM FEET, ANKLES, AND KNEES

Being able to adjust the tilt of your board on its edge is crucial to staying in control. The trick on ice is to keep balanced *over* the edge *as* you adjust its angle to the snow surface. The way to do this is through movements of your ankles and knees. Roll your ankles and push your knees toward the hill to increase the edge angle and "bite"; move them away from the hill to reduce the edge angle. Maximizing the

forward lean on high-back bindings lets you edge the board with less movement of your upper body. On ice, the closer to the board you make the edging movement, the better. Leaning with your upper body will cause serious problems.

GET LOWER ON ICE This gives you greater stability and lets you use your legs like springs to maintain contact with the snow. Focus on pushing and pulling your feet underneath you to make subtle adjustments to where you weight the board, rather than moving your trunk over the board. The latter requires more time and energy, and can lead to imbalance.

STEER WITH YOUR LOWER BODY Riding on ice mandates accurate and refined steering movements of the lower body. The upper body should remain stable and disciplined, and oriented in the direction of the upcoming

TUNING FOR ICE

When riding in icy conditions, make sure your edges are sharp and smooth. Razor-sharp edges are able to cut into ice and give you more "grip." Many racers bevel the full length of their side edges a few degrees to create a sharper angle that cuts into the ice better. Some folks leave the tip and tail at 90 degrees, and bevel their side edges a few degrees only in the middle of the board (usually between the feet). This enhances their grip on ice, without making their board "hooky" at the tip and tail. Keep in mind that if you bevel your edges, they will dull more rapidly than 90-degree edges, and that you'll have to file them more frequently to keep 'em sharp. More filing can mean shorter board life.

Even though it has a low coefficient of friction, some ice can be surprisingly abrasive, and can quickly "burn" the wax out of your base. Wax often to protect your board, and check your base after riding on an icy day: If you see white, dry-looking areas near your edges or in the base material, it needs to be waxed.

Work with an experienced shop or take a lesson on tuning. A well-maintained, properly tuned board will improve your performance on all snow conditions, enabling you to get the fullest potential out of your equipment and your abilities.

EDGE FROM FEET, ANKLES, AND KNEES Don't reach down on your toe edge on ice (1). When you reach down, your hips move back, effectively reducing the edge angle – and the amount you can "bite" your edge into the ice. Tilt your board on its edge using movements of your ankles and knees instead (2). This will get your edge to grip while keeping your body over the board.

ent: Your board works best when it's moving straight ahead. If you find yourself skidding out on ice, steer with your back foot so that the tail of your board once again follows the tip. Then concentrate on making carved (not skidded) turns.

ICE EXERCISES

Try the following exercises to develop unshakable ice-riding skills. Find a patch of ice on a gentle, wide, and uncrowded slope. Practice each exercise until you can perform it confidently and consistently.

turn. It should not be thrown around to try and generate turning forces.

SLICE THE ICE Snowboards work best on ice when they carve all the way through a turn. When your board slices through ice and hard snow, its construction allows it to absorb vibration, and your edge is better able to grip. Think of it this way: If you are driving on ice and your car goes into a skid, you steer into the skid to get all four wheels moving in the same direction. On a snowboard it's no differ-

VARIABLE-SPEED SIDESLIPS From a stop, sideslip at ultraslow, medium, and fast speeds. Work on maintaining a constant speed for extended durations. Practice on both toe and heel edges until you can select and maintain a desired speed, then shift gears from slow to fast, to medium, to a stop, and so on. Keep your upper body over your board; use your ankles and knees to edge the board.

STINGERS Make a series of short turns and

LOOK FOR SOFT, LOOSE SNOW

Most experienced ice riders know that ice occurs in patches surrounded by areas of softer snow. If an ice patch takes you by surprise, the best tactic is to relax, balance over the board, and use your edge to slow down in the softer snow downhill from the ice patch.

On busy trails, ride the sides. This will allow you to turn through deep accumulations of scraped-off snow, while others less knowledgeable are trying to navigate the icy middle of the trail. Lastly, use the sun to your advantage – especially in the spring when midday temperatures melt the snow surface, which then refreezes when crossed by late afternoon shadows. By riding the sunny sides of the trail, you are assured of the softest snow possible (that is, unless you're looking for ice).

see how fast you can decelerate as your board comes across the hill. Hit or "sting" the edge into the ice, then extend up and into your next turn. Practice until you can comfortably perform a series of turns to stops in balance.

The previous two maneuvers help you to control speed through the friction generated by skidding. But good ice technique requires both carved turns and skidded turns. Since there's less friction generated with carved turns, you must use the shape of your turns to decelerate.

SLICERS These will help you to eliminate skid — and chatter. Start with traverses. See if you can hold a high traverse with no sideways movement of the board. Practice until you can slice the ice consistently on both the toe and heel edges. No skidding! When you feel comfortable, progressively increase your angle of attack so that you start your slice closer to the fall line. Shape your slice by increasing the edge angle so that your arc brings you across and then up the hill, allowing you to decelerate and stop in balance.

SKID/CARVE TRAVERSES It is important to learn how to regain a carved turn from a skidded turn. Start by carving a traverse, then push the tail of the board downhill to start a

DO YOU LEAK?

To successfully ride ice, plug all energy leaks. Boots and bindings must fit and be adjusted properly, in order to efficiently transmit energy to your board. If your bindings do not securely hold your boots, adjust them. Check and tighten the adjustment screws on your bindings and boots often. Many boots and bindings come with mechanisms that allow you to custom fit them to your own body build and riding style.

The highbacks on many freestyle bindings can be rotated so that they run parallel to the board's heel edge, which allows for a greater use of leverage — and smaller movements — to create edging. Many highbacks also have mechanisms that allow you to adjust the amount of forward lean. Increased forward lean allows for quicker, more responsive edging to the heel edge, and enables you to edge using smaller (leverage) movements of the lower leg, rather than bigger movements of the hips or trunk. Of all the choices available, low-back freestyle bindings are the least responsive, because they don't allow you to use as much leverage to get your board up on edge. The ankle straps on soft-boot systems can often be adjusted to enhance energy transmission to the toe edge: The farther up your ankle the strap fastens, the better.

Three-strap bindings and many hard boots have channels on the inside ankle that allow the cuff of the binding to flex in that direction. While some riders enjoy the freedom of movement that this feature builds into the boot or binding, it does not allow you to effectively transmit energy to your equipment. Tighten it, and check it often! If you ride with high-stance angles, it's helpful to adjust this cuff cant outward on the rear boot, which will enable you to transmit a more powerful and responsive movement (more leverage) to your heel edge.

Some hard boots feature soft rubber soles that enhance traction in lift-loading areas and around the base lodge. These rubber soles are subject to abrasion and wear, especially if you go on lengthy expeditions wearing your snowboard boots. Check them often, and adjust the binding tension to take up the slack caused by sole wear. When the soles develop significant wear, or they become rounded, replace them. You'll get much better energy transmission, with no play between the boots and bindings.

STAY CENTERED Carving while keeping your weight over the board is the way to go on ice. The rider in the photograph on page 104 is too far off to the side and is headed for a belly slide.

becoming a virtuoso on ice.

TILT AND GO This is the exciting part. Tilt the board to engage your downhill edge at the start of the turn. If your snowboard is moving forward, with no sideways movement, engaging the downhill edge will pull you smoothly and effortlessly into a turn. Best of all, your forward momentum will allow your edge to grip like never before. Practice making long turns until you're able to connect sliced turns on both the toe and heel edges. If you feel yourself starting to lose your edge grip, recover the slice by pulling up with the rear foot as you did in the previous exercise. Then move smoothly into your next turn. When you feel comfortable and can slice the ice with consistency, have fun exploring variations in the size, intensity, and rhythm of your turns, and proceed to steeper, more slippery slopes.

Learning how to ride ice requires practice and patience. Remember, ice is one of the most demanding of conditions, and mastering these techniques often requires substantial time and effort. However, the satisfaction of learning how to ride ice safely and efficiently is well worth it.

skid. Pull the rear foot back so that the tail of the board once again follows the tip, and arc a clean line through the hard snow. Mastering the ability to recover from a skid is one key to

FreestyleBasics

your guide to the park, pipe and more

9

FreestyleBasics
your guide to the park, pipe and more

Freestyle riding is one of the most exciting (and certainly *the* most visually spectacular) aspects of snowboarding. Images abound of riders performing a dazzling array of acrobatic maneuvers on the ground and in the air. Worldwide, more freestyle boards and bindings are sold than any other type, and winter resorts are accommodating the burgeoning interest in freestyle riding by building half-pipes and terrain parks in which riders and skiers can "air it out."

PREREQUISITES You've *already* performed some basic freestyle moves, such as 360-degree spins and riding fakie while traversing. Even so, before you head to the park or halfpipe, you should be able to link turns comfortably on all blue (intermediate) trails.

RIDING FAKIE

One of the cornerstones of freestyle snowboarding — and a great way to continue to develop key movements — is riding fakie. Being able to ride fakie (or switch, as it is sometimes called) allows you to perform exciting spin tricks on the snow and in the air, and adds versatility to your snowboarding. Here's how:

1. Start on a wide, well-groomed green-circle (beginner) slope. Traverse the slope fakie (with your rear foot leading). Look in the direction that you want to go.

2. Weight your lead foot. In this case, because you're going backward, your lead foot is your *rear* foot. Steer the tail of the board (which, again, is leading) down the hill.

3. Make a smooth edge change in the middle of your turn.

4. Continue steering the board through the turn's finish. This is accomplished by performing the same techniques you used when

Two common problems often occur with first-time fakie riders:

1. They frequently weight the wrong foot as they attempt turns. Perhaps because they have devoted so much time to weighting the front foot to ride forward through a turn, they bring the same movement pattern into their first fakie forays, and, thus, have a tough time initiating and finishing turns. Remember to weight the lead (rear) foot through your fakie turns.

2. They often make an edge change too early in their first fakie turns, resulting in a body-pounding wipeout. Remember, timing is everything. During your inaugural fakie turns, be sure to make a smooth edge change in the middle of your turn.

It's tempting to revert to going forward whenever the terrain or snow conditions get difficult, but if your heart is set on becoming a proficient freestyler, don't. Going forward is forbidden. Make fakie your focus for an entire run — or for a series of runs.

making turns going forward: Twist the lead foot in the direction you are turning, and push the rear foot away from the direction of the intended turn. Make smooth, gradual movements and try to guide the board through a round arc in which the tip follows the path of the tail.

FAKIE TO THE END Force yourself to ride fakie for an entire run, even when snow conditions get tough.

5. When you've shed some speed by steering across the hill, repeat the process to turn on your other edge.

6. As you develop confidence and control, explore linking fakie turns, and changing the rhythm and size of your turns. Progress to steeper slopes and more challenging snow conditions as you develop consistency riding fakie.

Tip Rolls

It's not difficult to perform a tip roll to change from forward to fakie. To do so, you change to fakie by rolling off the tip of your board, which stays on the snow. After some practice, you'll be able to smoothly roll off the tip from

THE LIFT FAKIE

If you really want to master fakie riding, try using the lifts fakie. Keep your rear foot instead of your front foot in the binding as you get onto and off of the lifts. (Make sure you switch the safety leash to the rear binding before you do this.)

BASIC AIR Start small and progress to larger jumps as you improve. Approach the jump at a reasonable speed, with your weight centered and your hands in your field of vision. As you go off the jump (1), stay balanced over your board – don't let the jump kick your board out from underneath you. Look ahead and stay relaxed while you enjoy your flight (2), focusing on the area just beyond your landing. Get your board parallel to the slope (3), and bend your legs to absorb your landing (4). Ride off in search of your next jump.

inch, then 3 inches, and progressively higher, until you're balanced completely on the tip of the board. Both feet should be off the ground — you should feel pressure along the top of your rear foot and on the sole of your front foot. The tip of the board should be the only thing touching the ground.

3. Now try jumping and swinging the tail back and forth. You'll use this move to swing the tail of the board around when you perform a tip roll. Increase the amount that you swing the tail, toe side to heel side.

4. Continue swinging the tail farther and farther around.

5. Practice this movement so that you can consistently jump from one edge to the other, pivoting off the tip of the board.

Now apply the tip roll while in motion as you change from forward to fakie.

1. Start by traversing a gradual slope on your toe edge.

2. Throw your weight forward, twist your upper body in the direction you want to spin, and swing the tail of the board around *uphill*.

3. Roll 180 degrees off the nose.

4. Land on your heel edge.

5. Ride away fakie.

Throughout the maneuver, keep your body over the board and look in the direction you

forward to fakie — and off the tail to transition back to forward again. It's helpful to learn the tip roll on a flat surface area.

1. Slowly move your hips so far forward that the tail of the board comes off the ground (lift up with your back foot to help pull the tail off the ground).

2. Start small, lifting the tail of the board 1

want to go. As you practice, see how high you can lift the tail of the board as you roll off the tip. Once you develop consistency performing this maneuver, reverse the process to roll off the tail as you change from fakie to forward.

BASIC AIR

Catching air is one of the most exciting moves in all of snowboarding. It is the closest many of us will ever get to escaping the confines of gravity, albeit only briefly. To get the most from your snowboarding experience, take to the air, but make good decisions about when and where to do so, and how "big" to go.

TERRAIN If the area at which you're riding has a terrain park, start there. Terrain parks are designed to help you catch air. They usually contain a variety of structures on which you can practice, including ones that are specially designed to accommodate riders new to terrain parks. If the area does not yet have a park, any wide, uncrowded slope that has a variety of small rollers and berms to jump off of will do. If in doubt, ask a local rider, patroller, or instructor where to go.

FREESTYLER'S LANDSCAPE Terrain parks can include a wide variety of features, such as jumps, rail slides, and halfpipes. This type of curved track is called a snake run.

STANCE ANGLE AND RIDING FAKIE

Most avid freestylers ride with low stance angles. Having both feet positioned across the board allows you to easily ride in either direction. While it is possible to ride fakie with higher stance angles, it is a bit more difficult and feels more awkward (you feel like you're truly going backward). If you intend to specialize in freestyle and fakie riding, adjust your stance angles accordingly.

1. Inexperienced aerialists often crash on landing because they were not balanced on takeoff. As you ride over a jump, try to stay over your board. Take into consideration the profile of the takeoff ramp as you prepare to jump (don't let an irregularly shaped ramp throw your body backward or to the side), and spring straight up. Good landings are the result of balanced takeoffs.

2. Beginners often look down when they launch to gauge their landing. This throws them off balance and makes a crash landing inevitable. Look ahead throughout the jump: during your launch, while sailing through the air, and during your landing. This allows you to jump and land in balance, and to quickly spot your next jump.

Your First Air

Don't start by jumping the huge cliff you've been eyeballing all season, or immediately going to the biggest hit in the terrain park. Start on flat ground. Spring straight up — not off to either side of the board — and bend your legs deeply to absorb the landing. Pogo while waiting in line and before you take off at the top of the lift: it'll help you practice jumping and landing in balance and warm you up in the process. Then, on your descent, look for a small jump (4 to 6 inches high). When you find it:

1. Approach the jump at a reasonable speed.

2. Look ahead, and keep a quiet upper body. Make sure that your hands are in front of you, in your field of vision.

3. As you hit the top of the small jump, gently spring *straight* up.

4. Stay over your board. Look ahead, not down at your board.

5. Enjoy your flight.

6. Bend your legs to smooth (absorb) your landing. Ride out of the landing zone.

7. Look for the next jump.

DROP-OFFS AND JUMPS

When first learning the delights of catching air, it's important to know that there are two different types of "jumps." Knowing the characteristics of each will allow you to quickly become an air master.

Drop-offs This is where the slope suddenly steepens. As the name suggests, when you travel over an abrupt change in pitch, your momentum carries you forward (often into the air) as the slope drops away beneath you — and suddenly you feel light. Drop-offs do not redirect the momentum of your body as jumps do, and for that reason many people find it easier to stay in balance while learning to catch air by starting on small drop-offs. Extreme riders (after careful inspection of the site, snow conditions, and landing area) occasionally launch off 60-foot cliffs — big drop-offs indeed!

Jumps These are natural or man-made ramps in the snow. As you travel over a jump, the shape of the terrain redirects you upward. Therefore, you will need to be prepared for this change in direction. Most of the features found in terrain parks are different types of jumps, including tabletops, spines, kickers, and quarterpipes and halfpipes. The shape of the takeoff ramp, combined with your speed and how much and in which direction you spring determine your trajectory — and the types of acrobatics best suited for that particular jump.

ance. Explore a variety of grabs and contortions: using your front or rear hand; and grabbing the tip, tail, toe, or heel edge of the board.

AERIAL SPINS

The following advanced freestyle moves take time and practice to master, but if your focus is on freestyle, these moves are necessary, in order to perform even more advanced (and fun) freestyle tricks. Experimentation and repetition are key.

Jump 180s

After becoming comfortable with fakie riding and basic airs, you can combine them by throwing in a 180-degree spin while in the air. A jump 180 is the first step toward

JUMP 180 (FORWARD TO FAKIE) As you traverse the slope, crouch down on your toe edge (1) getting ready to spring. Your upper body should be wound slightly in the direction opposite the one in which you'll spin. Twist your upper body in the direction you're spinning and spring — and spin — off your edge (2). Spin your board 180° in the air (3) while looking slightly past your landing area. Land (4) on the heel edge, bending your legs to absorb the landing. Continue turning as you ride away (5,6) fakie. Do not make the classic beginner's blunder of stopping immediately after you throw the move. Freestyle snowboarding should be a seamless flow from one maneuver to the next. Keep going!

GRABS

After you become comfortable jumping, you can gain extra style points by grabbing your board while in the air. As you jump, it's vital that you bend your legs to bring the board up to your hand, rather than reach down to the board, which will put you badly out of bal-

more complicated aerial spins, and allows you to connect freestyle tricks forward to fakie — and back again. Here's how it's done:

1. Start by riding a fakie traverse on your toe edge across a gradual slope.

2. Crouch low before you jump, and "wind up" your upper body in the direction opposite

the one in which you will be spinning.

3. Spring straight up (if you have too much weight off to the side, you'll wobble like an unbalanced wheel).

4. As you start to spring up, uncoil your pre-wound body to initiate the spin. Keep your arms bent at the elbows and pointed in opposite directions (toward 6 and 12 o'clock), to enhance balance and prevent wobble.

5. It's crucial to spring and spin off your edge: You cannot generate spin off a flat board or while in the air. Try not to let the board skid out from beneath you on takeoff.

6. During the middle of the spin, look in the direction you're spinning. As you are completing the spin, look in the direction you'll be heading after you land.

7. Land on your heel edge riding forward. Absorb your landing by deeply bending your legs.

8. Practice. When you can jump — and land — 180s fakie to forward, try them forward to fakie.

9. Once you can spin jump 180s from your toe edge, try them from your heel edge, fakie and forward.

HALFPIPE DESIGN AND TERMINOLOGY

The best halfpipes are built to very precise specifications and are regularly maintained by special groomers. Like baseball parks, which provide a venue for a specific activity but change configurations from city to city, halfpipes at different areas have unique characteristics: some are steeper, some are wider, some have higher walls. Enjoy diversity – go to lots of baseball parks; ride in lots of halfpipes.

HALFPIPE SPECIFICATIONS

TECHNICAL DATA		MINIMUM	RECOMMENDED	MAXIMUM
	Inclination	15°	18.5°	22°
L	Length	100m	110m	120m
W	Width	13m	15m	17m
H	Wall height	3m	3.5m	4m
T	Transition	4m	5m	6m
V	Vert		.03m at 85°	
B	Bottom flat		5m maximum	

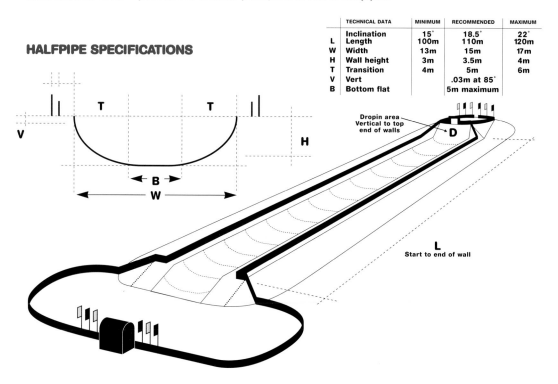

Dropin area
Vertical to top end of walls

D

L
Start to end of wall

HALFPIPE ANATOMY
Although each halfpipe will have its own feel, there are specific parameters that all competition pipes must meet. These are the specifications that Olympic athletes must train to.

360s

After developing proficiency in jump 180s, try a full rotation in the air while going forward. The movements are the same ones executed in spinning a jump 180, except you need to wind up and rotate your body more forcefully, and land on the *same* edge, going in the *same* direction as when you started. It's a great idea to practice on flat ground, with your snowboard off: jump, spin, and land — in balance. (Think of the possibilities — you can now practice your freestyle moves at the office water cooler.)

Once you feel confident in your ability to spin 360 degrees (and land) in balance on flat ground, grab your board, hit the slopes, and try it on a traverse. When you've mastered a 360 spin on a traverse, try it off a small jump. Progressively increase the size of your jump and your air time as you gain confidence. Then try spinning in the opposite direction, spinning in the park and in the pipe, and combining spins with grabs. The possibilities are endless (and loads of fun).

RIDING THE HALFPIPE

In the United States, halfpipe events have attracted the largest audiences in the history of *any* organized ski competition. Halfpipe riding is one of the two Olympic snowboarding events (the other is the giant slalom). Increasing numbers of areas feature halfpipes that are made entirely out of snow and regularly maintained with special grooming equipment. Halfpipe

riding is fun and easy when you take a step-by-step approach. Here's what you need to know to get started:

PREREQUISITES To ride the pipe you should be able to link turns on all blue trails. Riding the high walls found on the sides of many trails allows you to duplicate some of the situations — and sensations — you'll encounter in the pipe. Proficiency in fakie riding, basic airs, and carving will ensure you better balance, greater versatility, and more fun your first time in.

TERRAIN Often areas build minipipes for beginners. Smaller and often less crowded than a regulation halfpipe, they provide a great learning environment for first-time pipe riders. If the area at which you're riding has a minipipe, head there first. Otherwise, go for the big one (the halfpipe).

Ride the Transitions

First, learn to ride the transitions (the area between the wall and the bottom of the pipe) on a single edge. The falling leaf will help you to control your speed and direction as you adjust to climbing and descending the walls of the halfpipe.

When the pipe is clear, enter at the top. Keep your speed in control by avoiding the elevated starting ramp (if there is one). You'll be ready for it soon enough.

1. Stand tall as you traverse the bottom of the pipe and bend your legs as you climb the wall on your toe edge.

FRONT-SIDE AND BACK-SIDE WALLS

Your stance determines which is your front-side and which is your back-side wall. For goofy riders, as you stand at the top of the pipe, the left wall is the front-side wall and the right, the back side; for regular riders, the opposite is true.

2. As you slow to a stop on the wall, shift weight to your rear foot, look over your rear shoulder, and ride down the wall fakie, toe edge. Balance over your board as you transition off the wall and ride across the flats.

3. Reverse the process on the opposite wall.

4. Repeat the process on your heel edge.

5. Start slow. Keep a shallow angle of attack during your first few times through, and progressively increase your speed, to climb higher up the wall.

6. Perform the falling leaf until you are comfortable riding up and down the walls on either edge.

Turns on the Wall

The next step is to make a series of turns on the wall. Start by riding low on the walls; increase your height as you develop confidence.

1. Compress your body as you ride up the transition.

2. Extend your legs to start your turn.

3. As you turn, smoothly change edges and ride back down the wall.

4. Compress as you ride up the transition on the opposing wall.

5. Extend, and turn again.

Jump Turning

Next, try jump turning on the wall.

1. As you begin to decelerate on your way up the wall, spring up and turn your board in the air.

2. As you jump, twist your upper body slightly in the direction of the turn.

3. Land on the wall on your other edge.

4. Absorb the landing by bending your legs and balancing over your board through the pipe's transition.

5. Compress your body as you ride up the

opposing wall, jump, and turn.

6. Repeat until you can jump turn consistently on either wall, or until your legs give out.

It helps to carve across the bottom of the pipe and up the walls. Carving allows you to hold a higher line (and with it, delight in more "hits"), and carry speed better. If you hike the pipe between runs, examine your tracks. Are they carved or skidded? Does the line you select allow you to maximize the number of times you climb (and jump) the walls? More hits = more tricks = more fun.

Going above the Lip

After you become comfortable riding and jumping on the walls, explore carrying your speed up the wall and out of the pipe.

1. Drop in from the elevated starting ramp, where more experienced riders start. Carve across the bottom of the pipe.

2. Compress as you ride the transition and carry speed up the wall.

3. As you reach the lip, spring straight up (in the direction that the vertical section of the wall is carrying you).

4. As you begin to spring, twist your body in the direction that you want to turn.

5. Pull your front foot slightly toward your chest as you take off.

6. Turn in the air above the lip. Look for your landing spot while in the air.

7. Bend your legs as you land on your other edge to absorb the landing. You want to land on the wall, not low on the transition or the bottom of the pipe (ouch!).

8. Carve across the pipe and launch off of the next wall.

As you practice, strive for balance and consistency on both front- and back-side walls.

GOING ABOVE THE LIP Compress as you ride up the wall **(1)** getting ready to spring off the lip. At the top of the wall, spring and turn your board in the air **(2)**. Ideally, your hands should be in front. Compress as you land **(3)** and ride down the wall (this rider is staying on his toe edge; if he turned more in the air he would've had to land on his heel edge). Ride up the next wall and repeat. And repeat. And . . .

ADVANCED HALFPIPE RIDING

Once you are comfortable riding the walls, turning, and performing basic airs in (and above) the halfpipe, you'll want to take it to the next level. Advanced halfpipe riding requires that you be able to connect a smooth sequence of maneuvers on the front- and back-side walls from the top to the bottom of the pipe.

You can build a strong foundation for advanced halfpipe riding by practicing jump 180s in the pipe. This maneuver is also known as a "half-caballerial" or "half-cab," named for skateboard champion Steve Cabellero, who perfected fakie 360-degree spins in the halfpipe.

1. Enter the pipe on your toe edge and hit the front-side wall.

2. Just before you spring off the wall, twist your upper body in the direction you're going to spin.

3. Spin 180 degrees and land on your heel side, riding down the wall and across the pipe fakie.

4. Ride fakie up the next wall on your heel edge, and as you launch off the wall, spin 180 degrees and ride down the wall toe side.

When you are able to connect front-side airs to fakie and back-side half-cabs, try reversing the sequence. Enter the pipe on your heel edge and hit the back-side wall. At the top of the lip, spring, spin 180 degrees, and ride down the wall on your toe edge fakie. On the next wall, throw a half-cab (fakie to forward), and ride down the wall on your heel edge. Practice jump 180s until you can perform them forward and fakie on either wall.

WHICH DIRECTION TO SPIN?

When performing spin tricks you have two options: You can spin by rotating in the direction of your toe edge or in the direction of your heel edge. Try both to determine the direction in which you're most comfortable spinning. Practice spinning in both directions to get the most from your freestyle riding.

Half-cabs give you the foundation to launch — and land — every conceivable spinning aerial maneuver. Judges in competitive halfpipe events evaluate variety, difficulty, amplitude, rotation, and execution. You may not be training for a halfpipe contest, but keep these things in mind as you focus your training.

When riding the pipe, think ahead. Know what you're going to do on each hit *before* you get to the top of the wall. You can use the shape of particular sections of pipe to your own advantage. Just as when choosing a line in the bumps, you can let the terrain assist you in performing a trick. You'll develop an eye toward what sections are better for what types of maneuvers as you practice.

SAFETY, JUMPS, AND YOU

Before you jump, keep these safety considerations foremost in your mind:

Look before you leap Do *not* jump unless you are absolutely sure that the landing area is clear. Don't jump in "family" or "slow" zones.

If you can't see the landing area, enlist the help of a spotter He will tell you when the landing area is clear.

Inspect the jump – and the landing area – before you launch. Don't jump until you are familiar with the landing and snow conditions.

Avoid jumps with flat landings Sloped landings are much gentler on your body.

Never stop under a jump Ride out of the landing area before stopping to watch your friends. If you happen to fall, get out of the landing zone as quickly as possible.

Go small before going "bigger than life" Most snowboarding injuries occur when boarders attempt maneuvers beyond their abilities. Don't let your friends or your pride make you do something you're not ready for.

Steeps:
BlackDiamond
&Beyond

when the riding gets near vertical

10

Steeps: BlackDiamond & Beyond

when the riding gets near vertical

of riding the slope. This is true for advanced-level riders as well as beginners.

It's important to remember that steep is a relative term: To a beginner, a green-circle trail may be terrifyingly steep; to an expert rider, black-diamond terrain may not be steep enough. The techniques discussed here for handling steep terrain are appropriate for beginners as well as experts. They can be used *whenever* you feel the slope is too steep, but I'll define steep as a black-diamond slope — one on which you'll tumble, or slide, to the bottom if you don't ride it proficiently.

Before you hit the steeps, warm up with three simple but helpful exercises on a moderately pitched slope:

LEAPERS Jump to initiate each turn. Ride a series of long-turn leapers and short-turn leapers.

TAIL-RETRACTION TURNS Move your body forward over the board's tip at the beginning of each turn, and lift the tail of the board through an aggressively steered turn.

SHORT TURNS WITH EDGE SETS Link rhythmic, short turns down the fall line with your goal being a forceful edge set at each turn's finish. Go for big spray!

One of the most profound joys in learning to snowboard is advancing to progressively steeper terrain. The feelings of exhilaration and accomplishment that accompany the successful completion of a descent are almost as exciting (and at least as long lasting) as the fun

STEP-BY-STEP STEEPS

PREREQUISITES You can link short, rhythmic turns on all blue (intermediate) and easy black (expert) trails. You are comfortable with going fast and can come to a controlled stop quickly, on either edge.

TERRAIN Find a slope that is steep and wide, with soft, relatively smooth snow. As is the case when learning anything new on your snowboard, the terrain you select is crucial to your success. To learn to ride steeps, you have to practice on steep terrain. Don't, however, attempt your first-ever descent down a rock-studded, ultrasteep, icy chute overhanging a cliff. Practice first on wide, steep sections that are clear of obstacles and have good runouts.

Developing Speed Control

Gravity is by far the biggest factor in contending with steep slopes. On such terrain, you'll accelerate through a turn like never before, and it is critical that you are able to quickly slow down through the turn's finish. The trick: Work with gravity, not against it. It's a good idea, at this point, to revisit those first moves you relied on to control your speed on moderate slopes.

SIDESLIPPING Practice sideslipping on both your toe and heel edge. Start slow and work toward moderate-to-fast speeds. Push your knees and hips toward the hill while keeping your upper body oriented in the direction of your next turn. This separation of the upper and lower body helps you to balance, aids in edging, and creates a coiled area at your waist that, when uncoiled, helps you to steer smoothly through your next turn.

TRAVERSING Once you gain confidence in your ability to control your speed by sideslipping, try traversing and making forceful edge

STEEPS are whatever slopes on which you feel challenged. As you develop experience and technique, you'll undoubtedly progress to even steeper slopes.

sets. See how quickly you can stop. As you set your edge, sink down by bending deeply, with your knees and hips toward the hill. This will help you to balance through a quick deceleration. As in sideslipping, your upper body should be facing in the direction of your next

SIDESLIP THE STEEP Sideslipping is a great way to develop control and confidence on steep slopes.

turn (that is, if you are going to make one).

Practice sideslipping and traversing to an edge set until you can stop quickly and in balance on either edge. Try to leave a definite mark in the snow as you set and release your edge.

FALLING LEAF AND GARLANDS To control your direction as well as your speed, perform the falling leaf maneuver (alternately going forward and fakie) and garland turns. Remember that you can *always* use these moves to descend ultrachallenging slopes.

As you practice, increase your speed from moderate to fast by using less edge angle. In-crease your angle of attack, each time steering your board a little farther down the hill. Intensify the steering movements of your legs to quickly direct the board down and then across the hill. On steep terrain, you don't want to spend too much time with your board pointed straight down the fall line: The quicker you can steer it across the hill, the easier it will be to manage your speed.

TO MAKE THE TURN

1. From an edge set, extend your body *away* from the slope, toward your new turn. Frightening as it may seem (at first), this movement into the turn is crucial to making good turns on the steeps — it allows you to work with gravity, rather than against it.
2. As you extend away from the slope, your board will become light and you can quickly and easily turn it (which, on steep terrain, is important).
3. Make aggressive steering movements with your legs to guide the board through the turn and across the fall line.
4. Sink down as you finish the turn by driving your knees and hips toward the hill. This will help you to balance and to set your new edge. Your upper body should be stable and facing the direction of your next turn.
5. When you feel comfortable, repeat the extension move away from the hill to start your next turn. Sound athletic? It is!

This steep turn is straightforward and bombproof. It features sound fundamentals that will allow you to ride the steepest black-diamond trails with confidence and ease. The application of key movements will vary somewhat as pitch increases and snow conditions become more challenging.

TO MAKE THE TURN From a slightly crouched position (1) with your board across the hill, extend out from the slope (2) to make your turn. This key concept is called "maintaining perpendicularity" because to do it, you must keep your body perpendicular to the slope. As you extend, use your legs to quickly steer your board through the turn and onto the new edge. You will quickly accelerate to amazing speeds if you keep your board in the fall line for too long, so turn it fast. Bend your legs (3) as your board comes across the hill to absorb the forces of your deceleration. Repeat the same sequence to the other edge (4-6). When the slope becomes even steeper, you'll want to jump your turns from one edge to the other.

DEALING WITH FEAR

It's natural to experience fear when in a situation that is potentially dangerous. At no time does snowboarding feel more dangerous than when you're standing at the top of a near-vertical slope. What if you can't stop? What if you crash? What if you get hurt — or worse? These thoughts may come to you as you stand at the top of a steep pitch, and can interfere with your performance. Here are some of the symptoms of fear, and ways to deal with them:

MUSCLE TENSION When you are afraid, your muscles tense up. It's much harder to perform the movements necessary to ride a steep slope (bending your knees, for example) if your muscles are stiff and tense. Before

LEAPING CORNICES Make sure that the cornice is stable and that the landing area is clear. Then go for it!

1. Riders often experience chatter when finishing a high-speed heel-side turn. This occurs because they don't flex their legs enough to work with the forces caused by deceleration. You can avoid this by bending your legs through the end of your turn. While waiting on lift lines and during heel-edge traverses, practice sinking as low as you can on your heel edge. Remember to stay over your edged board (don't allow your bending legs to bring your body out to one side of the board), and sink low.

Try jumping and landing on your heel edge while traversing the slope. This movement duplicates the forces you'll experience when cutting a hard heel-side turn. Land softly by bending your knees after each jump. Practice until you are able to jump and consistently land in balance on your heel edge.

2. On steep terrain, snowboarders often twist their upper body toward the center of the turn that they are on (toward the hill). Called overrotation, it will prevent you from balancing, setting your edge, and quickly and easily starting your next turn. On steeps — and elsewhere — orient your upper body toward your *next* turn, not the one you're on.

starting down a steep pitch, shake out your key muscle groups and gently bounce up and down in place. This helps to relax the muscles that you need to rely on by moving them in a manner similar to how you'll move as you ride. Twist your torso, shoulders, and neck before starting to ride to warm up those muscles. Think loose.

RAPID PULSE, SWEATING, AND RAPID, SHALLOW BREATHING While you may not be able to immediately change your heart rate or the amount that you perspire, taking a few deep relaxation breaths can help to alleviate these physiological symptoms of fear. Try this breathing exercise now: Exhale deeply, from your abdomen, then inhale deeply and slowly, drawing the breath deep into your belly. Feel good? It's no accident that Zen masters use breathing exercises to clear their minds of distracting thoughts (such as the perception of danger). Breathing deeply also oxygenates your blood — plus, it makes you feel good. If you are on the slopes and begin to sweat and feel your heart race, practice this breathing exercise, and repeat until you are totally tranquilized.

FOCUSING ATTENTION ON THE PERCEIVED DANGER Like a deer frozen in the headlights of an approaching car, we are apt to zero in on a perceived danger (the tree, the cliff, or the lift tower), instead of where we are heading, when riding the steeps. It's crucial to focus on where you want to go, and on what you want to do. It's helpful to give yourself one or two cues to focus on when you're riding. Rather than think, "I hope I don't fall over that cliff," think, "Ride a high traverse to the top of that unbelievably sweet chute."

NEGATIVITY AND SELF-DOUBT If you *think* that you won't be able to ride down a particular slope, you probably *won't*. But most likely you *can* snowboard down almost any slope at any ski area or winter resort. Give yourself a vote of confidence before starting out. It makes a big difference.

A FINAL NOTE Ironically, sometimes we are motivated by fear to do things that scare us. The fear of "losing face" in front of a group sometimes can push people into doing remarkably stupid things on a snowboard. Don't let this happen to you. All of the positive thinking and relaxation exercises in the world won't do you a lick of good if you don't first develop the basic skills to ride the steeps, and work within your limits. Don't allow friends — or pride — to convince you to try a slope or steep chute that you're not ready for. Remember, it's important to *progressively* increase the amount of challenge, rather than to go for it all at once. When your friends say "Go!" don't be afraid to say "No."

STEEP CHUTES Riding chutes can be as exciting — and as challenging — as snowboarding gets. Select easy chutes with good runouts first and progress to steeper, narrower, more-thrilling chutes as you improve.

SPECIAL SITUATIONS
Steep Chutes

Chutes are steep, narrow paths of snow that run between rock outcrops. Riding them is one of snowboarding's most thrilling challenges (watch virtually any snowboarding video and you'll see footage of pros riding chutes). Here's how to get to know chutes:

- Start with friendly chutes — ones that have an "out" if you need it. You should be able to make short-radius turns and hop turns on steep ungroomed slopes before venturing into the chutes.

- When you are in a chute, the slope can be so steep that you can't see the area you're riding into. Know the area: Scout out the entire run before you jump in, and memorize it.

- On steep chutes, be alert for falling ice, snow, and bodies. Keep in mind that avalanches kill people.

- Don't stop in the middle of a chute: Ride to a safe area at the bottom before stopping.

Leaping Off Cornices

Cornices are overhanging masses of snow that form to the leeward side of a ridge. While leaping from cornices can be a great thrill, keep in mind that these structures are very unstable. Mountain resorts work to ensure that each cornice within area boundaries is safe, and will not bury you in an avalanche if you decide to ride over it. Even so, only venture onto a cornice when you are absolutely sure that it will not fall. Here are a few tips for your first cornice drops:

1. Don't air a cornice blind! Know the height of the drop — and whether there are people or obstacles below it — before you launch. Remember that cornices usually form over steep slopes.

2. Start with small drops and gradually increase the height as you gain expertise. Find a place on the cornice where you are comfortable, and can see your landing.

3. Work into the fall line gradually. It's often easier to first air a traverse. Do not shoot the fall line at high speed until you are comfortable leaping off the cornice from a traverse. Know your landing, including snow depth and conditions, traffic patterns, and the location of any obstacles.

4. Redirect your board in the air, pushing the tip down and retracting your rear leg slightly, so that the board parallels the landing slope. It also helps to retract your legs during the launch, so that you do not hang up your tail.

5. Don't turn in the air. Keep your board going in the same direction as it was when your took off (knowing how to air is, obviously, a prerequisite).

6. Don't go off sideways. Maintain forward momentum.

7. Don't stand at the top and think about it for too long. If you've made the decision to go, you have the skills necessary to do it safely, and the landing is absolutely, irrefutably clear — GO FOR IT!

8. Once you land, don't immediately stop to admire your tracks or to watch your friends. Clear the landing area and find a safe, highly visible place to stop. Then congratulate yourself!

Backcountry Basics
rediscovering the roots of riding

11

Backcountry Basics
rediscovering the roots of riding

ibility that snowboarders received as they rode at Alpine resorts. Now snowboarding is one of the fastest growing sports in the world (not to mention an Olympic sport), with most of the popular attention focused on resort riding. All along, though, backcountry purists have continued to climb and ride, pushing limits far from the eyes of the general public. In some ways, snowboarding has come full circle: As the sport's popularity explodes, many people — searching for untracked powder, solitude, and wonderful new experiences — are discovering for the first time the joys of snowboarding in the backcountry.

Backcountry boarding offers a unique experience that combines elements of climbing and mountaineering with off-trail riding. Far from the commotion and bustle of a downhill resort, backcountry boarding often brings you to the best snow conditions: deep, untracked powder. Best of all, you'll discover an intense natural experience, encountering animal tracks and untrammeled wilderness vistas. Backcountry riding is good for your soul.

While this chapter provides useful information that will get you thinking about riding in the backcountry, the subject goes far beyond the scope of this book. Learning to safely negotiate the challenges posed by the backcountry is a lifelong endeavor. An excellent,

Snowboarding got started by hardy, impassioned people eager to hike up snowy hills to ride back down on primitive equipment. As boards evolved, increasing numbers of ski areas allowed the newcomers on their slopes, and rapid growth came with the increased vis-

comprehensive guide to backcountry pursuits is *Mountaineering: The Freedom of the Hills* (The Mountaineers). Get a copy of this remarkable book, keep it by your bed, and read it. The information you absorb will help you to fully (and safely) enjoy each one of your backcountry outings. It may come to pass that in an emergency, you'll be glad you did.

The bottom line in the backcountry is that you are responsible for your own safety. At a winter resort, high-mountain hazards are controlled. In the backcountry, however, there is no one to blast threatening cornices and loaded snow slopes; no one to place ropes or signs to help you to find your way around sheer cliffs; no one to mark the location of rocks, stumps, or other obstacles lurking underneath the snow surface; and no one to rush to your rescue should you injure yourself. It's up to you and your partners to navigate safely. Do not go blindly into the wild: What you don't know *can* hurt or kill you. Take a course, or learn with *experienced* friends. You'll find the challenges and rewards of backcountry snowboarding to be well worth the training and the risks.

CORN SNOW You'll encounter a wide variety of snow conditions in the backcountry, including some you'll never see if you ride exclusively at resorts. This rider is enjoying late afternoon light on spring corn snow.

RIDING WITH A PACK

Riding with a loaded pack can affect your balance, so practice on gentle terrain before you try it on steep slopes. Use cinch straps to snug the load as close to your back as possible, and fasten shoulder and waist straps tightly (the only exception is if you're riding a suspected avalanche slope — you'll want to be able to jettison your pack quickly in the event of a slide). Keep upper-body movements to a minimum as you turn. The momentum of a swinging pack can easily throw you off balance.

As you carry larger and heavier loads to more remote destinations, you'll probably want to establish a base camp near where you'll be riding. This allows you to leave bulky or nonessential items, such as your tent, stove, food, and sleeping bag, behind, while you ride for the day.

PACK RIDING (OPPOSITE)
Be careful when you ride
with a loaded pack. The
extra weight can easily
throw you off balance.

PREREQUISITES Before you head into the backcountry, you should be able to ride a wide variety of ungroomed snow conditions and challenging terrain in control. Additionally, you should have training and experience in backcountry exploration.

TERRAIN Any slope off the beaten track. Riders new to the backcountry may want to start with simple off-trail treks and dayhikes, and progress to multi-day expeditions as they gain experience in winter camping, avalanche awareness, route finding, technical climbing on high-angle snow and ice, and other backcountry skills.

Before You Go

Prepare! This is the best way to ensure a safe and satisfying backcountry boarding experience. Research your destination and alternate routes. Make informed estimates on how long it will take to get out and back safely. Tell your friends where you're going, your intended route, and your estimated time of return. If you don't call them by a prearranged time, they should initiate a search. You may want to pad your estimated return time, however, to cover unplanned delays, but don't pad it too much. You need to make realistic, informed estimates and meet them.

Check the long-range weather forecast, and bring along enough gear to allow you to comfortably adjust to the *worst* weather that may occur while you're out. Keep in mind that in the mountains, weather changes can be sudden and severe. Since local avalanche conditions may differ from forecasts, it is prudent to call the local avalanche hotline to help assess the risk of snowslides for the area in which you're traveling.

BACKCOUNTRY GEAR
Packs

To carry the accoutrements of backcountry riding, you could use very deep pockets or a shopping cart. However, neither would allow you the freedom to move quickly and easily over rugged landscape. A well-fitted pack, sized to your particular needs for any given trek, is a much better solution. From a lightweight daypack to a full-size expedition backpack, it's helpful to use a system expressly designed for moving gear in the backcountry.

LUMBAR PACKS offer light weight and compactness. They fasten around the waist, and are the perfect choice for a quick half-day ascent and ride. You can lash your board to the outside of the pack and use an additional lash strap fastened around your shoulders and the tip of the board to keep it from moving around (see "Lashing Your Board to Your Pack," page 136). Even the most generously sized lumbar pack will only be able to transport enough gear for a short hike, however. If you'll be out any longer than half a day, use a backpack.

DAYPACKS are useful if you're hiking near a road or trailhead. They can carry enough gear to get you out for a good day of riding when the weather is nice. Packs that feature ice ax

PACK IT IN, PACK IT OUT

It's up to all of us to keep the backcountry pristine. Pack out *everything* that you packed in. Also, try to pack out any trash that other, less-thoughtful people left behind. Leave only footprints and broad tracks!

PACK IT IN A lumbar pack (1) is the perfect choice for a half-day ascent and ride. A daypack (2) accommodates enough gear and food for a one-day outing. A full-sized pack (3) is best if you plan to spend one or more nights in the backcountry.

loops and lash anchors allow you to fasten extra gear to the pack's exterior. Look for sturdy, padded shoulder straps, a waist belt, and a sternum strap for the utmost in stability while hiking over rough terrain and while riding. Do not overstuff your daypack. If you need to carry extra gear, bring a larger pack. **FULL-SIZE BACKPACKS** are best if you're carrying heaps o' gear (say, for an overnight trip). Internal-frame packs that hug the back and can be cinched down tight to stabilize the load and keep a low center of gravity work best. Look for sturdy construction: reinforced wear areas and stitching, storm flaps over all zippers, sturdy and well-padded shoulder and waist straps, and loops and anchors on the outside to fasten extra gear. Full-length side zippers (along with carefully planned packing) allow you to get at often-needed items without having to unstrap your board or dig through the rest of your gear. Buy your pack from a reliable outfitter that prides itself on hiring knowledgeable, experienced salespeople who can help make sure your pack fits: An ill-fitting pack will cause you untold misery on the trail.

Loading a Pack

Do not simply dump your gear into your pack and roar off into the wilderness. Take a moment to carefully load your gear into your pack. You want to create a balanced load

LASHING YOUR BOARD TO YOUR PACK

Use your pack to carry your board while hiking. You'll need two 36-inch or longer lash straps (available at any outdoor shop) and a little creativity. Use the compression straps on the sides of your pack or any handy external lash anchors to fasten your board to the back of your pack. Thread the straps through your bindings to keep your board from sliding down. Fasten it as low and as close to your back as possible to ensure easy, balanced hiking; yet high enough so that it won't hit your legs (especially as you hike down hills).

that's easy to carry and allows you easy access to your gear while en route. It's best to load the heaviest items at the bottom, close to your lower back, and to load the lighter items higher up toward your shoulders. This will keep the weight over your hips and legs, providing optimal balance. An unbalanced, top-heavy pack will be extremely difficult to carry, and can throw you off balance at the worst possible time — such as during a delicate crossing of a log over a glacial-fed torrent (see "Riding with a Pack" page 133). It's helpful to wrap all gear that isn't waterproof in plastic bags, in case you don't quite make it across that icy torrent. Loading a pack is an art: You'll find that you develop your own unique system as you gain experience.

The Ten Essentials

What, exactly, should you put *in* your pack? "Be prepared" is perhaps the best advice when it comes to tackling backcountry challenges. While you may not need each one of these items while hiking that roadside powder patch, you'll find them enormously helpful — and possibly lifesaving in an emergency. Carry them with you whenever you hit the backcountry.

1. MAP AND COMPASS Carry a topographic map of the area (in a waterproof protective case, such as a Ziploc bag) and a compass to help you navigate in the backcountry. You can use them to determine your location or to plot your route — and to find the quickest way out in an emergency. Carrying a map and compass does not guarantee that you won't get lost, however. You need to learn how to use them.

2. WATER AND WATER BOTTLES Don't succumb to dehydration on a peak. Carry an ade-

ESSENTIAL ATTIRE Even during late-spring hikes into the backcountry, always bring along an outer shell and hat. The weather can change fast in the mountains.

quate supply of water with you (approximately 2 quarts a day per person; more on strenuous climbs or at high elevation). Use insulated carriers to keep your water from freezing. They lash nicely to the outside of your pack for easy access. To quickly supplement your water supply, you can use the water in your jug to help melt snow. Put a couple of handfuls of clean, fresh snow into your nearly full

EYE PROTECTION Goggles are a must if snow is in the forecast. They offer protection from snow, wind, and ultraviolet rays.

jug to keep a water shortage at bay for a few additional miles.

Make sure you use a water filter or purifier if you take water from lakes or streams, and bring a stove to melt snow on longer, colder expeditions. Be alert for human or animal waste that could contaminate a water supply (and be especially careful that you do not contaminate any water source when *you* go).

3. FLASHLIGHT OR HEAD LAMP WITH SPARE BULBS AND BATTERIES Night comes on fast during the short days of winter. Be prepared. Carry batteries separate from the flashlight: This will prevent your light from accidentally being switched on (and your batteries being drained) while in your pack.

Lithium batteries hold a charge best in cold temperatures.

4. FIRST AID KIT Take a wilderness first aid course, and bring a first aid kit with you on *all* backcountry trips (basic or expedition size, depending on your destination). Commercial kits are widely available, although you may want to supplement the contents to suit your needs.

5. EXTRA FOOD You burn more calories to stay warm in the winter. Since you don't want to run out of gas miles from the trailhead (especially if circumstances force you to stay out longer than you had planned), it's a good idea to bring along an extra supply of lightweight, nonperishable energy foods such as GORP (good old raisins and peanuts), power bars, nuts, and dried fruits.

6. EXTRA CLOTHING Every summer, climbers die of "exposure" (hypothermia), because all they brought to a summit were the clothes on their back. Summer or winter (and anytime in-between), bring along extra layers including a hat and a windproof, waterproof shell to keep you warm and dry in case the weather changes. Expect change, and be prepared.

7. SUNGLASSES Harsh ultraviolet (UV) rays (which at 10,000 feet are 50 percent greater than at sea level) can sunburn your retinas, a painful condition known as snowblindness. Since clouds do not block UV rays, you need to wear eye protection even when it's overcast (backcountry boarding is much more fun when you can see). Use high-quality, UV-blocking sunglasses or goggles. Glacier glasses work especially well at high elevations. On extended trips, carry spare eyewear in case someone in the group breaks or loses theirs.

8. POCKET KNIFE Swiss Army-style knives or pocket multitools such as the Leatherman enable you to do far more than spread peanut butter. They are indispensable for equipment repair, fire starting, and first aid, as well as for food preparation. For all blades and tools, stainless steel is best.

9. MATCHES, IN A WATERPROOF CONTAINER An emergency supply of matches should accompany you on all backcountry treks. On extended trips you'll need to melt snow and cook using a stove. In an emergency, building a fire could save your life.

10. FIRE STARTER Matches alone will not ignite wet wood. Bring along a fire starter (such as a candle, stove fuel, or commercially available heat tabs) to quickly build a warming fire in an emergency.

These are the absolute, essential basics. Depending on your destination and length of journey, you probably will need to bring along additional items.

Other Essential Gear

AVALANCHE BEACON/PROBE/ SHOVEL If you are in avalanche country, make sure that everyone in your group has a beacon (transceiver), probe, and shovel, *and knows how to use them*. Regular practice in search-and-rescue using the transceiver could save a life (see "Avalanche Safety," page 142, for more information).

EXTRA SUNBLOCK Sunburn hurts, and can cause long-term health problems, such as skin cancer. Use a sunblock with an SPF of 15 or higher for snowy environments. Keep in mind that snow is highly reflective: Apply sunblock to *all* exposed skin, including the underside of your nose, ears, and chin. Don't forget your lips: Use an SPF-rated lip balm, to avoid sunburned lips (and the feeling that you kissed a hot skillet). Reapply sunblock periodically throughout the day for maximum protection.

AVALANCHE BEACON If you're heading into avalanche country, every member of your party must carry one of these lifesaving devices.

WHICH BOOT?

Unfortunately, the perfect backcountry boot has yet to be made. So, do you go hard, soft, or mountaineering? There are advantages and disadvantages to each:

Soft boots are easy to hike in, and work especially well when hiking or riding powder. They also work well with most snowshoes and are comfortable. They don't work as well, however, for kicking steps or for riding steep, icy slopes.

Hard boots are great for kicking steps into steep, hard snow, and fit easily into snowshoes, backcountry skis, and crampons. They also provide better purchase on icy slopes than soft boots, but don't work as well when hiking, especially over talus slopes and rocky trails.

Plastic mountaineering boots are a good choice if you expect a challenging approach hike or climb. They work well for kicking steps, and fit easily into crampons, backcountry skis, and snowshoes. The ones that have a Vibram sole are great for hiking over bare ground, rocks, and talus. Because they are not specifically built for snowboarding, however, you can expect some performance trade-offs with mountaineering boots. You decide.

GOGGLES If there is any possibility that it could snow, bring goggles. They'll protect your eyes from falling snowflakes better than standard sunglasses, and often come with interchangeable lenses that allow you to adjust to changes in lighting.

ICE AX/CRAMPONS Both of these will ensure greater safety and security on steep, exposed, icy slopes. Learn how to use them and practice. They're more dangerous than helpful in untrained hands.

SNOWSHOES If you're facing a long approach hike through deep snow, snowshoes are the way to go. The folding models are great, because they save space in your pack.

REPAIR KIT You'll want to carry an emergency repair kit for your equipment, which includes extra binding screws, tape, wire, pliers, needle and thread, and patching material.

HELMET When climbing a steep chute where falling rock or ice is a possibility or where you could tumble a long way if you fell, a climber's helmet is a great idea. It can also work to protect your noggin on the snowboarding descent.

THE ASCENT

Use snowshoes or backcountry skis if your approach is long and through deep, untracked snow (lash them to your pack during your descent). You may choose to climb without them if the ascent has already been bootpacked or if you'll be hiking during the late season on hard, frozen snow. Telescoping ski poles are very helpful no matter what you have on your feet. On those extra-long approaches (if you're lucky enough), a snowmobile, airplane, or helicopter ride can come in handy.

Start out very early in the morning and you'll guarantee yourself the longest amount of daylight possible. During the late season you may enjoy firm, refrozen snow in the early morning hours. Then, as the sun warms things up, you may find that the crust you skimmed over on your last ascent has turned to hip-deep glop that can be excruciatingly hard to hike through. Solar energy can also weaken once-safe snow bridges, trigger rock and ice falls, and set off wet-snow avalanches. Work with the sun. If you time your hike well, you'll enjoy fast, efficient hiking over frozen snow, and a silky smooth descent on a surface layer recently thawed by the sun.

If there is no packed trail to follow to your destination, take turns breaking trail (unfortunately, first tracks aren't as exhilarating on the way up as they are on the way down). Hiking through deep snow can be an amazingly intense workout. If you're hiking without snowshoes, look for areas of hard snow, in order to stay on top of the surface. The harder snow often appears as a slightly different shade of white. You may also notice areas in which the snow is less deep or packed by winds, such as the windward side of a ridge. If available, walk in preexisting tracks to help save energy. However, in avalanche country, on glaciers, or on cornice ridges, do not blindly follow in someone else's tracks. Snow conditions continually change, and what was once safe could turn dangerous.

Take It Slow

Pace yourself on your approach, using a steady, methodical, measured stride rather than short, intense sprints that will inevitably lead to out-of-breath, exhausted rests. At higher elevations you'll find it helpful to coordinate your breathing with your steps, using a rhythmic pattern: step, breathe, step, breathe.

Shed your gear before you get hot and sweaty. Drink frequently and nibble energy snacks as you go. If you need to stop, get off the trail so that others behind you do not have to posthole through loose snow to get around you.

Be Alert

Don't just plod along with your head down. Continually monitor your route, being alert to any potential hazards such as avalanches, falling rocks and ice, dangerous cornices, hidden crevasses, tree wells, or partially covered streams (while simultaneously enjoying the spectacular views and unforgettable scenery that surrounds you). Keep a safe distance between you and the person ahead of you, and look out for loose rocks or chunks of ice or snow that they may inadvertently send down onto your head. (Also be ready to dodge *them*, if they slip and fall.) As you reach your destination, take the time to savor the rarefied air of the summit (if conditions permit) before descending.

The Best Part – The Descent

Although the ascent in a backcountry riding experience has many rewards — including a terrific workout in a beautiful natural setting (endorphins!); the enjoyment of collaborating with friends to meet the challenges of navigation through a wintry landscape; and the peace and solitude that accompany any wilderness experience — the best part is yet to come: the descent. Whether you float down through an

STAY ALERT Be as careful on the way down as when climbing. Avalanches, falling rocks and ice, unarrested falls, and glacial crevasses can hurt you just as badly when you're riding.

expanse of untracked powder or surf through spring corn, you'll be delighting in some of the best turns you've ever made. Take the time to stop occasionally, and admire your tracks and those of your friends.

Have fun as you ride, but always be alert to hazards. The same challenges you faced on the

FASTEN BINDINGS WHERE IT'S FLAT

If you'll be riding a steep slope, fasten your bindings *above* the steep part. Attaching bindings while clinging to a near-vertical wall is difficult and spooky – if you lose your balance and tumble with the board half attached, you could be seriously injured. If you can't find a flat area, create one using your shovel, ice ax, or boots.

AVALANCHE ALERT Masses of powder accumulated on steep, open slopes can lead to avalanches. Avoid such areas.

obstacles. Stay together as a team to ensure that all members get down safely. Besides, riding together allows a *shared* peak experience.

A single run in the backcountry is usually better than an entire day of riding at a ski area. Backcountry runs will be among the best, most memorable rides you'll *ever* have on your snowboard. Each run in the backcountry is an ultimate, unforgettable experience!

BACKCOUNTRY SAFETY
Don't Go It Alone

While there is much to be gained from the solitude that the backcountry offers, it's more enjoyable — and much safer — to go with friends. On a multi-day trek you can split up shared items, such as a tent, any climbing gear, and food, to make your load lighter. It's a good idea to rope up on steep, exposed sections and definitely while crossing glaciers. Your life may depend on the experience of your friends, so choose your partners wisely. You'll be especially glad of their training if they happen to arrest your fall into a glacial crevasse or dig you out after being buried by an avalanche. In an emergency, traveling in a party of three will allow someone to stay with an injured person while the other goes for help. In addition to these worst-case rescue scenarios, the best part of traveling in a group is that you get to share the experience with friends.

Avalanche Safety

Avalanches are the number one hazard faced by backcountry travelers, whether they are traveling on snowboards, skis, snowmobiles, or snowshoes. There is no substitute for expert instruction and hands-on experience in the field. If you'll be boarding in avalanche

way up (potential avalanches, falling rocks and ice, overhanging cornices, glacial crevasses) are still present — and just as hazardous — on the way down. Deep powder can also cover rocks, stumps, tree wells, and other

country, study books and videos on avalanches and *take an avalanche course*. A good course will teach you when and where avalanches are likely to occur, how to avoid them, what to do if you're unfortunate enough to be caught in one, and rescuing others who have been caught in a slide.

Some basic rules:

● Stay out of the backcountry during times of high avalanche danger.

● Recent snow and wind or big fluctuations in temperature increase the chance of sliding snow.

● Everyone in the group must carry and know how to use an avalanche transceiver, probe, and shovel. Transceivers should be double-checked to ensure that they are in "transmit" mode before heading onto suspect terrain.

● If possible, stay off avalanche-prone slopes. Stick to heavily forested areas and ridge lines, if possible. Slopes of 30 to 45 degrees (about the pitch of steep, black-diamond slopes) are most likely to slide, although other slopes can be prone to avalanches also. Signs of past avalanches indicate a slope has a history of sliding.

● Put on gloves and warm clothing and loosen your pack straps (in case you need to jettison your gear) before you venture onto a potential avalanche slope.

● If your group is on a suspect slope, expose only one person at a time to the potential danger. That person must move quickly, but gin-

BACKCOUNTRY BUDDIES In addition to all of the compelling safety reasons not to go it alone, the best reason is that you get to savor the experience with friends.

gerly, until he is out of the zone.

● Climb straight up a suspect slope instead of cutting across it (the action of crosscutting could trigger a slide). If you *must* traverse, stay as high on the slope as you can.

● Work as a team, and clearly communicate your intentions before moving.

If You're Caught in a Slide

● Yell so your partners know what's going on.

● Try to stay on your feet if you can and get to the side of the slide. Forces and speeds are less intense at the slide's edges. You're unlikely to outrun a slide, even on your board:

TAKE A FIRST AID COURSE

A knowledge of wilderness first aid can save your (or a friend's) life. A good resource is *Mountaineering First Aid*, by Marty Lentz, Steven C. MacDonald, and Jan D. Carline (The Mountaineers). The best option, however, when it comes to developing skills in wilderness first aid is to take a course. Check with local colleges, outdoor supply shops, your local ski patrol, or the Red Cross to locate the course that's right for you.

AVALANCHE RESCUE Fast, decisive action is the key to rescuing a buried avalanche vicitim. Do not go for help if you witness someone being buried. If the area is reasonably safe, find and uncover the victim yourself using your transceivers, probes, and shovels. Never venture into avalanche country without these lifesaving tools. Practice and master search-and-rescue techniques before you need to use them. You – or your friends – may be glad you did!

Large avalanches have been clocked at well over 80 miles an hour.

- Throw off your pack, poles, and whatever else might weigh you down under the surface of the moving snow, as quickly as possible. Unfortunately, this becomes problematic if you are caught while riding, as you cannot quickly release your board (all the more reason to be cautious).
- Do whatever you can to stay on the surface.

Many survivors have had success using a swimming motion.

- Quickly pull your goggles down over your mouth to prevent snow from blocking your airway.
- As you feel the slide slow, make your greatest effort to reach the surface. You'll be unable to move any part of you that's buried after the snow stops.
- Before the snow stops, use your arms or tuck your jaw down into your jacket to create a breathing space. This is extremely important because you'll need air until you can be rescued.
- Remain calm if you find yourself buried. Conserve your strength and precious oxygen as you await rescue. (You weren't out there alone, were you?)
- Yell *only* if you hear rescuers very close by: The snow will muffle your shouts, and your shouts will waste oxygen.

Avalanche Rescue

If you witness someone being caught in an avalanche, you need to act quickly and decisively. Do *not* go for help. Fast action is often the difference between life and death.

- Mark the place where the person was last seen, keeping an eye out for additional slides.
- Perform a quick search downhill from that

SNOWBOARD AS SLED

On long, gradual approaches, you can use your board as a sled to carry your pack and other equipment (particularly if you are lugging a fully loaded expedition pack). With your snowboard base down on the snow, lash your pack through your bindings and fasten a line to the haul loop at the top of your pack (you'll find it between and slightly above your shoulder straps). You can attach this line to a hip or chest harness for hands-free hauling. You'll find it's much easier to break trail to your distant destination without a 60-pound gorilla on your back. Keep the shoulder straps facing up. That way, if you need to put on your pack to carry it across a bare section or during a stream crossing, you'll be ready.

spot. Look for any obvious clues, such as clothing, equipment, or blood, that could provide important information regarding the whereabouts of the victim.

- Turn your beacons to "receive" and perform a systematic search of the area. If your group has practiced using avalanche beacons, you should be able to locate the burial location in minutes.
- Carefully probe the target area.
- When you locate the buried victim, dig him out as quickly as possible using your shovels.

- Perform first aid as necessary.

Statistics show that most people (about 14 out of 15) survive being caught in an avalanche, usually because they're not totally buried. Only one person in four who is totally buried, with no clues on the surface, survives a slide. One third of all deaths by avalanche are caused by blunt trauma to

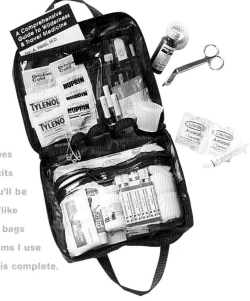

THE FIRST AID KIT

Your first aid kit should contain items that you will use regularly and ones you hope you'll never need to use. Prepackaged backpackers' first aid kits are available or you can assemble your own. Keep weight in mind – you'll be carrying your kit on all backcountry forays – but don't skimp on items (like bandages) that you will rarely use but are vital in an emergency. Ziploc bags let me organize the contents of my kit into items I use regularly and items I use only occasionally. Just be sure, if you put your own kit together, that it is complete.

Contents of a Sample First Aid Kit

- Names and numbers of people to contact in an emergency
- First aid report form to inform search and rescue party
- Blister kit (mine has Second Skin, 1-inch-wide medicine tape, moleskin, and a needle)
- Antibiotic ointment (Neosporin or Bacitracin)
- Hydrogen peroxide or rubbing alcohol for disinfecting (a 2- or 3-ounce plastic bottle is plenty)
- Space blanket
- Painkillers
- Rubber gloves, face shield for CPR
- Medicine tape (1 inch wide – doubles for repair on gear)
- Tweezers and scissors (your army knife may have them)

- Ace bandage
- Gauze (2-inch roll)
- Gauze pads: several 3-inch and 4-inch squares
- Band-Aids and butterfly closures
- Medicines: cold tablets, antihistamines, throat lozenges, Alka-Seltzer; if you're going on an extended trip, ask your doctor about prescribing a general antibiotic, and Flagyl too, if you're going to ignore the warnings in this chapter and drink unpurified water, Diamox for high altitudes
- Personal prescription drugs
- Extra moleskin
- Antidiarrheal medication
- Tincture of benzoin

the body. Being caught in an avalanche has been compared to taking a spin in a giant Cuisinart. In short, when it comes to avalanches, you can never be too careful. Always be alert for potential slides — avoiding an avalanche is far easier than surviving one.

Watch Out for Tree Wells

In deep powder, exert extra caution around evergreens, where you'll often find partially covered holes in the snow, called tree wells, surrounding the base of the tree. These are caused by overhanging branches that block falling snow and by scouring winds that swirl around the base of the tree, drifting the snow. Tree wells are often completely covered by a thin layer of snow. Be careful not to get too close to snow-cloaked evergreens. Through the years, several snowboarders have suffocated after falling into tree wells.

HIGH-MOUNTAIN HUTS

Along some established trails (most notably in the Colorado Rockies), high-mountain huts or yurts are available for use during winter months. These structures, typically located a day's hike from a trailhead, can be spartan or luxurious — sometimes including wood stoves, wood-fired saunas, hot water for showers, and comfortable furniture. The allure of these amenities, plus being surrounded by beautiful, untracked slopes, will make you want to extend your stay — or to return. Check with regional mountain or hiking clubs for additional information and to make reservations (you may need to reserve a spot well in advance).

TuningTips
keeping your boarding gear in top shape

12

TuningTips
keeping your boarding gear in top shape

slopes you think you're performing at your best. But you're not. Not if you don't regularly tune your snowboard. Whether you are a beginner or a serious competitor — or anything in-between — you cannot reach your highest levels of performance without regularly tuning your equipment. Don't neglect your equipment: it's well worth maintaining.

As with car maintenance, you can do a lot of the simple upkeep yourself. There are tremendous benefits to being self-reliant, and, if you're like me, you will derive satisfaction from working on your board. There are certain situations, however — such as regrinding your base or repairing a damaged core or edge — that demand the services of a trained technician. In these cases, bring your board to a reputable shop for repairs.

PREREQUISITES To tune your board, you need a dirty, banged-up, or out-of-tune board; a willingness to work with your hands; time; and patience.

TERRAIN The best place to tune your board is in a clean, well-lit, and ventilated area, which has a workbench, a vise to hold your board, and tuning tools. Many people use a fishing tackle box to store and organize their tuning equipment.

Imagine the perfect winter day. Two feet of fresh powder cover the surrounding peaks. You've worked out all summer, invested in the best equipment you can afford, and trained with a skilled snowboard coach. You're ready for this run. As you career down the glistening

MAINTAINING YOUR BOARD
Preparation
Clean the topsheet, base, edges, and sidewalls of your board with solvent and a clean rag

before you do any work on the base or edges. Dirt, wax, and grime hardens with time, so it's best to clean your board after each day of riding, especially if you transport your board exposed on a car roof rack.

I use citrus oil-based solvents (Citrus-Solve, Simple Green). They do a great job of removing the dirt and gunk without unduly harming the environment (or me). Once your board is clean, let it dry for 15 to 20 minutes so that any remaining solvent evaporates. Now you're ready to tune it.

Checking for a Flat Base

Your base needs to be flat. Use a straight edge or commercially available board-tuning true bar to make sure there are no high or low spots on your base. Use a bright light source behind the bar as you sight along the base and you'll be able to spot any surface irregularities.

If your base is higher than your edges, it's "base high." Base-high boards drift unpredictably when you are going straight, and make edging difficult.

If your base is lower than your edges, your board is said to be edge high or "railed." A railed board is hooky: The high edges tend to grab and send your board (and you) into an unexpected turn. Another way to check for

BASE GRINDING Get thyself to a reputable shop to have major repair work done on your board. This shop technician is grinding a board's base flat using a belt sander.

railed edges is to run your fingernails from your base to your edges. If you feel your nails catch on the edge, you do not have a flush surface where base meets edge — and, thus, your board is railed.

If your base is not absolutely flat, bring it in to a shop and have it ground. Check around locally to find out which shop has a stone grinder or belt sander (stone grinding is preferable), and which does the best work on snowboards.

Repairing the Base

Inspect the base for gouges and dings. Gouges that penetrate the board's core or damage the

TOOLS YOU'LL NEED

Base Repair
- Biodegradable base cleaner
- Drip repair candles
- Metal scraper
- Surform or other planing tool
- Rilling bar
- Emery or silicon carbide paper (100, 120, 180, and 220 grit)
- Sanding block
- ScotchBrite pads
- Wire brushes

Edge Care
- Whetstone or diamond stone
- 6-, 8-, and 10-inch-mill bastard files
- File guide
- Gummy stone
- Biodegradable base cleaner

Waxing
- Base cleaner and clean rags
- Waxing iron
- Waxes
- Plastic scraper
- ScotchBrite pads
- Wire or nylon bristle brush

edges need to be fixed by a qualified technician in a repair shop. If you find any minor impact damage, you can fix it yourself with a drip repair candle (available at ski shops). Here's how:

1. Place your board base up on a workbench in a well-ventilated room.

2. Light the candle with a propane torch or lighter. Be careful not to let the molten plastic drip onto your skin or clothes. Avoid breathing the fumes.

3. Hold the candle with the burning tip lower than your hand and spin it slowly. You'll see clear molten plastic drip from the tip. Catch the hot plastic on a metal scraper.

4. Drip plastic into the gouge. If you see dark smoke or carbon deposits at the burning tip of the candle, *don't* drip them into the gouge: They'll be forever imbedded in your board's once-beautiful base. Rub them off using the metal scraper.

5. Fill the gouge entirely with plastic. You may need to apply several coats to fill a deep gouge.

6. Fill all gouges on the base. Let the new base material cool and harden.

7. Gently scrape off excess plastic with a Surform planing tool and metal scraper.

8. Sand (again, gently) with 200-grit sandpaper to complete the repair. You want the repaired area to be absolutely smooth, flat, and even with the surrounding base.

Structuring the Base

After making necessary repairs, you may want to "structure" your base (i.e., create tiny grooves running tip-to-tail in the base that help your board glide better). You can adjust the size of the grooves for different types of snow. Larger grooves work better for warm, wet snow; smaller grooves work better on colder snow.

Use emery or silicon carbide paper, a rilling bar, or a wire bristle brush to structure your base. Brush in smooth, overlapping, even strokes from tip to tail. Be gentle — you want to groove only the surface of the base, not the interior of the board. Once you've structured the base, polish it (again from tip to tail) with a ScotchBrite pad to remove the loose fibers created by sanding.

Sharpening Edges

Your edges are the interface between your board and the snow. Smooth, sharp edges, combined with good technique, will make your board handle like a Ferrari; dull, rough

JUST WHAT *IS* THIS STUFF, ANYWAY?

During the spring as the snowpack starts to melt, you may notice a dark residue fouling your board's once-pristine base. This mystery goo is the accumulated residue of a season's worth of airborne pollutants, car and diesel exhaust, wax from skis and boards, and organic compounds from the trees. As the snow melts, all of the residues that were suspended in overlying layers collect on the surface.

As this gunk accumulates on your base, your board will slow down noticeably, sometimes stopping completely on gently pitched slopes. What can you do? Use a citrus oil solvent to clear the base of your board. You may need to do so once or twice during the day in late spring. You can usually find base cleaner and a rag at rental and repair shops, or the snowboard school. Once the base is clean, your board will return to its zippy old self.

edges will make it handle like a dump truck. To keep your edges in top condition, clean and sharpen them regularly.

You'll be working on the two exposed sides — base and side — of each edge. You may find it easier to position the board base up for base filing, and sideways in the vise (with the base facing you) for side filing.

1. Use a whetstone or diamond stone to remove any case-hardened areas on your edges. Rub it gently back and forth along each edge, keeping it parallel with either the base or side surface of the edge.

2. Run your finger gently along the edge to ensure that it's smooth.

3. Place your board base up on the workbench and flat file the edge along your base. Apply light pressure to the file as you draw it along the edge (see "The File File," below). Check with your finger to ensure that this part of the edge is smooth and flat.

4. File the sides of your edges to create a smooth surface and a sharp angle where base meets side. The edge should be sharp enough to scrape off the surface layer of your finger-

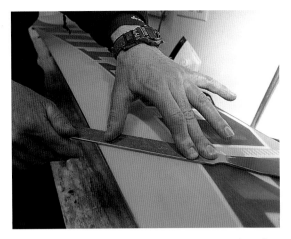

BASE FILING You can use the base of the snowboard to help keep your file flat when you file the base. Pull the file along the base, stopping to clean it frequently.

nail when you brush lightly against it.

5. If you want to bevel the edges (see "To Bevel or Not to Bevel," page 152), angle the file accordingly. Use a file guide for accuracy.

6. After filing to the desired sharpness, polish the edges with a gummy stone.

7. Detune the tip or tail if you so desire (see "Tuning . . . and Detuning," page 154).

8. Using solvent, clean the base of any stray filings or dirt.

THE FILE FILE

Files are precision cutting tools. Treat them right and they'll keep your board in top condition. Abuse them and your ride will suffer.

Choose a file appropriate for the task at hand. Files with large cutting teeth will remove a lot of material from your edge, and should be used sparingly and only for extra-large dings. Smaller-toothed files will remove far less material, allowing you many more tune-ups. Use them for small dings and touch-ups.

● As you file, clean the file of any accumulated metal frequently. There are special tools (called file cards) with which to do this.

● Files are made to cut in one direction only. You'll quickly damage a file if you use it in the wrong direction. Don't use a back-and-forth sawing motion when filing your edges. Pull or push the file in its intended direction, lift, and repeat as necessary.

● Special tools (called file guides) can be used to ensure that your file cuts at the same angle along the length of the edge. Use one to get precise-edge angles.

9. Always be careful with sharp edges: They can slice you or your clothes.

To Bevel or Not to Bevel

You can custom-tune your board by beveling its edges. When you bevel, you file the edge at an angle to either the base or sidewall. An adjustable file guide can help you to cut your edge so that it is beveled anywhere from 1 to 4 degrees on the base or side. Remember when you bevel to start small and increase the amount of bevel as necessary: You can always file off more edge, but can never replace the edge once you've filed it off.

Base beveling keeps your edges off the snow when your board is flat. Most board manufacturers and shop technicians bevel the base anywhere from 0.5 to 1.5 degrees. A beveled base can help beginners to learn and freestylers to spin with less likelihood of catching an edge. Some racers claim that beveled base edges allow them to glide faster because only the base is in contact with the snow. Other performance snowboarders keep their edge flush with the base so that they'll be able to engage their edge faster, with less overall movement of their body. This is useful anytime you need to get on and off your edge quickly, such as in the bumps, on ice, on steeps, and in quick slalom turns.

Side beveling adjusts the angle of the side of your edge. Most edges come from the factory parallel to the sidewall and perpendicular to the base. By beveling your side anywhere from 0.5 to 4 degrees, you can create a sharper angle (less than 90 degrees) on your edge, allowing it to better grip and hold on ice or hard snow. On the downside, if you're not careful, sharper-angled edges can mean slashed flesh and clothes. Beveled edges also tend to dull faster than 90-degree edges, meaning that you'll need to sharpen them more frequently, thus reducing the life of your board.

Waxing the Board

Regular waxing maximizes glide and makes it easier to turn and control your board. Wax when snow conditions change (such as when the temperature soars or drops), and anytime your base looks dry. Faint white lines or patches will appear on a dry base, especially near the edges. Since a dry base is more susceptible to damage and deterioration from UV rays, it is important to keep it waxed, in order to strengthen and protect it.

Do not wax your board if it's been sitting outside or in an unheated shed all night long. Bring your board in from the cold at least an hour before waxing to prevent damage to the base and to promote wax absorption.

1. Place your board base up on the workbench. Select a wax appropriate for the temperature range in which you'll be riding. Use a

EVERYBODY MUST GET STONED

Ever see sparks leap out from under someone's board when they strike a rock? The heat generated by sudden impact with a rock can change the temper of the metal edge, making it harder (this is called case hardening). Running a file along a case-hardened edge can damage it. Use a diamond stone or whetstone *first* to remove any case-hardened burrs along your edges, *then* file them sharp.

By the way, mountains are made of rocks. Carry your stone with you when you ride. If you happen to nick any rocks while en route, you can perform quick touch-ups to keep your edges smooth and sharp all day.

small cube of wax for easier handling.

2. Preheat the waxing iron (on low). You can purchase specially designed waxing irons from ski or snowboard shops, but a regular, retired clothes iron works equally well (just don't use it for clothes after you wax your board).

3. Adjust the temperature setting of the iron from low to medium, so that it easily melts the wax. Test the temperature by placing the wax against the iron briefly. If the wax smokes, the iron is too hot.

4. With the tip of the iron lightly touching the base of the board, melt the wax against the iron so that it runs in a thin stream onto the base. Move the iron in a pattern so that you leave a bead of wax that you can later iron into the base. When waxing, less is more. You ultimately want a thin layer of wax on the base, so go easy — you can always add more.

5. Place the iron flat on the base and keep it moving in small circles. Spread the wax bead out until the entire base is covered with a thin film.

6. The best wax retention is achieved through longer periods of ironing, so work back and forth along the base several times. Keep the iron moving: Long exposure to high temperatures will damage your base.

7. After the entire base is covered, allow the wax to cool and harden for 20 to 30 minutes.

8. Use a straight-edge or a plastic scraper to remove excess wax. Remove as much wax as

 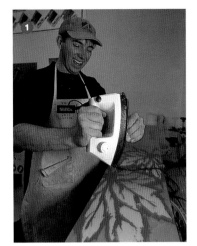

HOT WAXING – APPLYING WAX Use a hot iron to drip wax onto your base (1) If the wax smokes, the iron is too hot.

HOT WAXING – IRONING Keep the iron moving as you spread the wax over your base (2). Cover the entire base with a thin layer of wax. Continue ironing until the topsheet of your board feels warm (this extra ironing allows the wax to combine in a solution with the plastic in your base), then put your board aside for the wax to cool and harden.

you can, leaving a thin film to enhance your glide.

9. Polish with a ScotchBrite buffing pad so that your base is smooth and shiny. A well-waxed base should feel "soapy" or slick.

10. Finally, brush the base, using a nylon brush for cold conditions or a metal brush for warm conditions. Stroke from tip to tail.

A well-maintained board allows you to take full advantage of your athletic abilities *and* the design of your equipment. You'll notice the improved performance of your well-tuned board immediately, so go ride and enjoy!

MAINTAINING YOUR BINDINGS

Ever see a fellow rider walking down the side of the slope carrying his board because one of his bindings fell apart? It happens, it can ruin your day, and it can be prevented. Always check the nuts, bolts, and screws on your bindings *before* you head out on the slopes, and when you're tuning your board. The constant pounding and vibration of riding can cause these fasteners to become loose. Trust me, you don't want one of your bindings falling apart when you're at high speed in the steeps.

STORING YOUR BOARDING GEAR

You might find snowboarding so satisfying that you take up a nomadic existence, following the winter season and snow from the Northern to Southern Hemisphere and back again. Lucky you. If, however, you find yourself trapped on one side of the equator, you'll need to suffer summer and the accompanying deep snowboard longings. Until the start of the next "ice age," you'll have to store your boarding equipment through the summer months. Here are some tips to do it right:

1. Thoroughly clean your board with a cleaning solvent. Also clean your bindings and boots using the manufacturers' recommended cleansers.

2. After allowing the solvent to dry, apply a thick coat of warm-weather (yellow) wax to the entire base of your snowboard. Do not scrape this coat off until late next autumn — it protects your base during the summer.

3. Using a clean rag, apply a thin coat of machine oil to the edges to prevent them from rusting. Keep the oil away from the base and sidewalls.

4. Thoroughly dry your boots, and loosely stuff them with crumpled newspaper. If they're made of leather, remember to waterproof them before you ride next season.

5. Store all equipment in a cool, dry place. It's a good idea to store your board base up in an overhead rack, where it's protected and out of the way.

6. Have summer fun and pray for snow.

7. When it's time to ride, scrape the storage wax off the base of your board, and rewax appropriately for the late-autumn temperatures. Polish the edges with a Gummy stone, and hit the slopes!

TUNING . . . AND DETUNING

After you've filed your edge to razor sharpness, you may want to undo a bit of your handiwork. Detuning is the process of dulling the edges close to the tip and tail of your board. If you spin lots of freestyle tricks, or if you feel your board turns too quickly and unpredictably, round off your edges between 4 and 6 inches from where they contact the snow. However, if you like to carve – or race – keep the edges sharp tip to tail. This will give you the best carving power.

AASI Acronym for the American Association of Snowboard Instructors, an organization that trains and certifies professional snowboard instructors. Ask for an AASI certified instructor to be guaranteed a safe, fun, and effective snowboard lesson from beginning to ad-vanced levels.

ABS Acrylonitrile butadiene styrene is a tough plastic used to make snowboard topsheets, sidewalls, and (sometimes) bases.

Aerials Maneuvers performed in the air.

Air You breathe it and sail through it. You can't live for long without it. Jumping, or "catching air", on a board is the closest most of us will ever come to flying. It feels good and it's fun. Remember: "To air is human."

Angle of attack The degree to which you steer down the fall line as you ride across the hill. A shallow angle of attack is mostly across the hill and slows your decent; a steep angle of attack is the mostly downhill and hastens your descent.

Avalanche transceiver A small radio transmitter/receiver that should be worn by each member of a group traveling in avalanche terrain. The transceiver (also called a beacon) allows rescuers to quickly locate buried avalanche victims.

Backcountry Any place away from the slopes and lifts at a winter resort. The farther "back," the more "country" it is. Go far.

Back-side air Launching off your heel edge. The bigger the better.

Bail The metal piece that is used to fasten a hard boot to the binding. *Also*: to fall.

Base The bottom of a snowboard. Most bases are made of some type of polyethylene.

Bevel To file a slight angle into the base edge or side edge while tuning your board.

Big air What happens when you go off a big jump, also known as "catching big air." Big air contests feature competitors going off a tall (sometimes 35 to 40 feet) jump. Athletes are judged on height, distance, level of difficulty, execution, landing, and style.

Bindings Mechanisms that allow you to fasten your feet to the board. Bindings are built to accommodate either soft or hard boots.

Boardercross An increasingly popular snowboard event in which six competitors race simultaneously through a 3,000-plus-foot obstacle course featuring high banks and jumps. Although intentional contact is discouraged, racers often run into each other while trying to navigate the course. The first two competitors to complete the course advance to the next heat. The overall champion wins the final heat.

Booting out When your boots or bindings overhang your edges, they will hit the snow when you tilt the board high on its edge or when you ride a steep slope. You'll boot out — and undergo a body slide — when this happens. Position your bindings so that no part of them hangs over the edge (or use a fat board), and you'll never boot out.

Boots Hard or soft, boots keep your feet warm and dry. They also work to transmit energy to your board. Use boots that fit.

Camber The arch that is built into your snowboard (easiest to see when it lies on a flat surface). Camber works like an auto's leaf spring to distribute your weight along the length of the snowboard, making it easier for you to turn and making the board more stable at speed and on hard snow.

Cap A type of board construction where the topsheet of the board extends all the way to the edges. Sometimes the cap serves as a structural component of the board.

Carve A maneuver that uses the sidecut design of the snowboard to turn. When you carve, your board moves straight ahead so that its tip and tail pass through the same point in the snow, leaving a thin track in the snow.

Catching air See "Air."

Corduroy A type of snow surface created by grooming machines. Smooth and consistent, corduroy is an ideal surface on which to practice new or unfamiliar maneuvers. It's also great for blasting electrifying carved arcs.

Crampons Sharp metal cleats that fasten to your boots and provide traction while climbing ice and hard snow.

Downhill edge The edge that's farthest down the hill when your snowboard is across the fall line. Catching your downhill edge will result in a painful slam (which see).

Edge angle The amount that a snowboard is tilted on its edge. Being able to adjust your edge angle will allow you to control your speed. In a carved turn, adjusting your edge angle affects the shape of your turn: the higher the edge angle, the sharper the turn; the lower the edge angle, the longer your turn.

Edge change The action of smoothly moving from one edge to the other. The quicker the edge change, the sooner you'll start a new turn.

Edges Steel strips that surround the perimeter of your base. Sharp, smooth edges give you greater control on hard snow and ice.

Face plant A fall resulting from catching your toe edge (see "Slam").

Fakie Riding backward.

Fall line The most direct path down a hill. The path that a ball would take if you released it on a slope is along the fall line.

Flex How much, and where, a board bends. Freestylers typically look for softer, more flexing boards; carvers, for stiffer ones. Softer boards can be more forgiving but more difficult to control on hard snow or at higher speeds.

Forward lean The amount that a highback is angled toward the toe edge on a soft-boot binding. Most top riders use between a 15- and 25-degree forward lean to make powerful heel-side turns.

Freeriding All-mountain riding, including powder, bumps, trees, cruisers, jumps, and some tricks. Skilled freeriders can carve with abandon and ride the pipe too.

Freestyle Acrobatic riding that includes spins, airs, and other tricks. Freestyle snow-

glossary continued

boards are built specifically for freestyle maneuvers, with soft flex and turned-up tip and tail.

Garland A series of partial turns across the hill without edge changes, so called because the pattern they leave in the snow resembles a garland strung on a Christmas tree.

Giant slalom A timed competitive event in which racers turn around a series of poles (called gates) set in a particular configuration on the slope. Typically, giant slalom demands longer turns and higher speeds than slalom events.

Goofy Riding with the right foot forward.

Grab A freestyle move in which you hold a part of your board with your hand. You can grab the tip or tail of the board, or the toe or heel edge, and with your front or rear hand. This maneuver looks especially stylish while airborne and contorting.

Ground school Practicing — and mastering — key movements and basic snowboarding maneuvers on flat ground before applying them while on a slope. A little time spent in ground school will go a long way toward preventing wipeouts.

Halfcab or "half-cabellerial" An advanced halfpipe move also called a jump-180, named for skateboard champion Steve Cabellerio.

Halfpipe A U-shaped channel in the snow designed for acrobatic aerial maneuvers. A typical halfpipe is 300 feet long by 30 feet wide, with 6- to 10-foot-high walls.

Heel edge The edge of your snowboard under your heel.

Heel side A turn made on the heel edge.

Highback The part of a soft-boot binding that extends up from the heel cup behind the lower leg. Highbacks allow you to use leverage to create more powerful edging movements heel side.

Hit A jump.

Inserts The holes on a snowboard that hold the binding screws and allow you to adjust the position of your bindings.

Lip The top edge of the wall in a half- or quarterpipe.

Plate bindings Another name for hard-boot bindings.

Posthole Sinking up to your knees (or beyond) when hiking in deep snow. Postholing is both slow and exhausting, and is the primary reason why skis were invented.

P-Tex A manufacturer's product name for the polyethylene plastic used to make and repair snowboard bases.

Quarterpipe One-half of a halfpipe. A single wall with a smooth transition that allows a rider to go from flat to vertical — and then some.

Regular To ride with your left foot in front.

Safety leash A cord used to fasten your board to your leg or foot. Required by most ski areas, safety leashes help to prevent runaway snowboards.

Sidecut The smooth curve that's built into the side of your board from the tip to the tail. Sidecut helps your board to turn. Generally, the bigger the sidecut, the tighter you can turn.

Sideslip A maneuver in which you slide downhill with your board positioned perpendicular to the fall line. Sideslips are useful any time you feel overly challenged by a slope. They allow you to get out of trouble if you find yourself on difficult terrain or snow conditions.

Sidewall The material along the side of a snowboard that covers and protects its internal components.

Skating Propelling yourself across flats and up to lifts by pushing with your back foot, which is unclipped from its binding.

Sketch To have your snowboard slide out from underneath you when completing a turn or jump.

Skidding Moving your board sideways as well as forward. Skidding creates friction between your edge and the snow, which can help you to control speed.

Slalom A timed snowboard race in which competitors turn around gates set in a particular configuration on a slope. Slalom competitions demand fast, accurate turning; quickness; and great balance.

Slam The dreaded edge-catch wipeout. Seismic in nature, you can slam by catching your toe edge (face-plant) or your heel edge (spinal tap). Avoid slams by familiarizing yourself with edging movements.

Snurfer The first commercially sold snow surfer. The earliest Snurfers appeared in 1966 and were modified to become the forerunners of snowboards shortly thereafter.

Spinal tap A fall resulting from catching your heel edge (see "Slam").

Stance angle The angle of your bindings (and hence your feet) on the snowboard. Riders use high-stance angles (with the toes pointed toward the tip) for carving and racing. Low stance angles (with the feet positioned across the board) are more frequently used for freestyle and riding fakie. Freeriders generally ride somewhere in between.

Stomp pad An adhesive-backed pad that fastens to a board between the bindings. The stomp pad provides traction for the rear foot when skating and using lifts.

Switch Riding fakie on a twin-tip snowboard (because there is no tail — and no "rear" foot — which way is forward and which is fakie?)

Tabletop A type of jump that features a long flat area at the top of the ramp. Skilled riders clear the flat and land on the down ramp. Tabletops used in big-air contests for pros sometimes exceed 40 feet in heigth. Most terrain parks feature scaled-down versions.

Tail The back end of a snowboard.

Terrain park A specially designed area featuring different types of jumps and other fun features. Although first constructed to satisfy freestyle snowboarders, most terrain parks are open to all athletes, be they on boards or skis.

Tip The upturned part of the front of a snowboard.

Toe edge The edge of the snowboard underneath the toes.

Toe side A turn made on the toe edge.

Topsheet The material that covers the top of a snowboard.

Transition The smooth curve that connects the flat bottom of a halfpipe with its vertical walls.

Traverse To go diagonally across a slope, across the fall line.

Twin tip As the name implies, a twin tip has two tips (and no tail) and is used primarily for freestyle riding. The bindings are usually mounted the same distance from either tip, allowing you to ride with equal intensity in either direction.

Wall The side of a halfpipe. The backside wall is the one you'd hit on your heel edge if you were riding forward; the frontside wall is the one closest to your toe edge.

ASSOCIATIONS

International Snowboard Federation (ISF)
P.O. Box 5688
Snowmass Village, CO 81615
970-923-7669
http://www.isfna.com
http://www.isftechcom.org
http://www.deepcove.com/isf
http://www.isf.ch
The international governing body for snowboarding. Web sites include world rankings for competitors, rules, judging standards, event information, links, and message boards.

U.S. Amateur Snowboarding Association (USASA)
315 E. Alcott Avenue
Fergus Falls, MN 56537
http://www.usasa.org
USASA events encourage participation of all ages. Age brackets include Seniors (19-25), Master (26-35), Legend (36-49), Methuselah (50-59), and Fossil (60+). Check out this site if you are considering getting involved in local or regional competitions. The annual USASA National Championships bring together the best U.S. amateur competitors for freestyle and racing events.

U.S. Snowboarding
P.O. Box 100
Park City, UT 84060
801-649-9090
A governing body for organized snowboarding events and competitions in the United States.

American Association of Snowboard Instructors (AASI)
133 South Van Gordon Street
Suite 101
Lakewood, CO 80228
303-987-9390
http://www.psia.org
Offering ongoing training and certification for snowboard instructors, AASI provides manuals, videos, and on-snow clinics to teaching professionals. Noninstructors can order materials as well.

Canadian Snowboard Federation
2440 Place Prevel, Apt. #8
Sainte-Foy, Quebec
Canada G1V 2X3
418-688-9781

Ski Industries America (SIA)
8377-B Greensboro Drive
McLean, VA 22102
703-821-8276
National, nonprofit trade organization representing more than eight hundred ski and snowboard industry product manufacturers, distributors, and suppliers.

National Ski Areas Association (NSAA)
133 South Van Gordon Street
Suite 300
Lakewood, CO 80228
303-987-1111
http://www.travelbase.com/skiareas
Serves as the trade association for ski area owners and operators. Promotes on-snow sports and safety, and promotes the interests of the ski and snowboard industries.

The American Alpine Club (AAC)
710 Tenth Street, Suite 100
Golden, CO 80401
303-384-0111
http://www.gorp.com/aac/aachome.htm
Dedicated to disseminating knowledge about the mountains and mountaineering, and conservation and preservation of mountain regions and other climbing areas, the AAC library is the oldest Alpine research facility in the U.S. and has one of the largest mountaineering collections in the world, including books, photos, videos, journals, and maps. Check it out if you're planning a high-mountain snowboarding expedition.

BOOKS

Because the sport is so young, there aren't yet many comprehensive and useful books *specifically* about snowboarding. In addition to the snowboard listings, you may want to check out the Alpine ski books listed below. Because of the similarities between the two sports, it's often easy to extrapolate ski information to apply to snowboarding.

TECHNIQUE AND TACTICS

The Complete Snowboarder by Jeff Bennett, Ragged Mountain Press, 1994. This book provides useful information on snowboarding from beginner to advanced levels.

Snowboarding Know-How by Cristof Weiss, Sterling Publishing, 1993. Written for young adults, this book provides an overview of all aspects of the sport, from beginner exercises to freestyle tricks.

The Athletic Skier by Warren Witherell and David Evrard, Johnson Books, 1993. An excellent resource on canting and alignment (albeit for Alpine skis, it still gives you a good idea as to why custom configuring your alignment is so important). It also covers strength and flexibility training, and high-performance skiing technique.

Breakthrough on Skis by Lito Tejada-Flores, Vintage, 1986. A thoughtful and instructive book on how to ski to high levels of performance, this book covers technique and tactics for a wide variety of snow conditions and terrain.

High-Performance Skiing by John Yacenda, Leisure Press, 1987. A technical and psychological analysis of contemporary Alpine technique. Strong sections on getting the most from a lesson, sports nutrition, and fitness and conditioning. Includes sections on special skiing situations, such as bumps, steeps, powder, and crud. The text is well written, and reflects a passion for skiing that is spiritual as well as physical.

FITNESS AND CONDITIONING

Stretching by Bob Anderson, Shelter Publications, 1980. The recognized authority on stretching. Includes sport-specific groups of stretches for nearly every athlete.

Performance Skiing by George Thomas, Stackpole Books, 1992. A good, current resource on fitness and conditioning, flexibility, strength, cross-training ideas, technique, racing basics, and tech talk on equipment. Recommends specific and scientific approaches to training for skiing.

The Skier's Year-Round Exercise Guide by Thea Slusky, Stein and Day, 1979. Presents detailed information about muscle use in skiing, and suggestions for designing a specific personal training program. The Physical Fitness Quiz is fun, and revealing.

BACKCOUNTRY AND SAFETY-RELATED BOOKS

Mountaineering: The Freedom of the Hills Don Graydon, editor. The Mountaineers, 1992. The single most-useful book on mountaineering, climbing, and backcountry travel available. *Freedom* is the standard text for climbing courses throughout the U.S. and abroad. If your interests lie in off-trail explorations — or if you enjoy hiking, climbing, and backpacking, buy this extraordinary book.

Mountaineering First Aid by Martha J. Lentz, Steven Macdonald, and Jan Carline, The Mountaineers, 1990. A useful and easy-to-read guide on administering first aid in the backcountry.

The Avalanche Book by Betsy Armstrong and Knox Williams, Fulcrum Publishing, 1992. A well-written and informative guide on how to recog-

sources continued

nize avalanche terrain, and evaluate conditions that lead to stable or unstable snow; how to travel safely in avalanche terrain; survival and rescue techniques; and avalanche-control techniques. Includes riveting first-hand accounts from avalanche victims.

The ABCs of Avalanche Safety by Edward R. LaChapelle, The Mountaineers, 1985. A concise, pocket-sized guide to introduce the backcountry traveler to the basics of avalanche safety. This book will easily fit in your pack for consultation in the field.

Cold Comfort: Keeping Warm in the Outdoors by Glenn Randall, Lyons and Burford, 1987. Warm is good, especially in a decidedly cold environment.

Hypothermia, Frostbite, and Other Cold Injuries: Prevention, Recognition, and Prehospital Treatmant by James A. Wilkerson, C. C. Bangs, and J. S. Hayward, The Mountaineers, 1986.

Wilderness Skiing and Winter Camping by Chris Townsend, Ragged Mountain Press, 1993. Athough geared primarily to backcountry skiers, this information-packed book is an excellent guide to winter camping and backcountry travel. Check out the comprehensive gear list in the appendix.

TUNING AND EQUIPMENT MAINTENANCE

Waxing and Care of Skis and Snowboards by Michael Brady and Leif Torgersen, Wilderness Press, 1996. A comprehensive illustrated index on the hows and whys of equipment maintenance.

Alpine Ski Maintenance and Repair by Seth Masia, Contemporary Books, 1987. Although an Alpine ski tuning manual, this book presents a lot of information that is useful for tuning a snowboard.

MAIL-ORDER SOURCES FOR BOOKS AND GEAR

Adventurous Traveler Bookstore
28 So. Champlain Street
Burlington, VT 05401
800-282-3963
E-mail: books@atbook.com
http://www.gorp.com/atbook.htm
Search their full selection of more than three thousand titles by keyword. Largest supplier of worldwide adventure travel books and maps.

Backcountry Bookstore
P.O. Box 6235
Lynnwood, WA 90836
206-290-7652
Books and videos on all outdoor activities, as well as knowledgeable staff.

Campmor
P.O. Box 700-B
Saddle River, NJ 07458
800-CAMPMOR
Everything you need to outfit yourself for the outdoors.

Climb High
1861 Shelburne Road
Shelburne, VT 05482
802-985-5056
Full line of backcountry and mountaineering gear.

Patagonia Mail Order
1609 W. Babcock Street
P.O. Box 8900
Bozeman, MT 59715
800-638-6464
The finest in outdoor clothing.

REI (Recreational Equipment, Inc.)
1700 45th Street
Sumner, WA 98390
800-426-4840
Snowboarding and outdoor equipment, classes, and clothing.

Reliable Racing Supply, Inc.
643 Upper Glen Street
Queensbury, NY 12804
800-274-6815
Providing high-performance ski and snowboard accessories and clothing. Not just for racers.

Sierra Trading Post
5025 Campstool Road
Cheyenne, WY 82007
307-775-8000
Mail-order discounts on discontinued gear and factory seconds. Great deals, but limited selection.

Tognar Toolworks
P.O. Box 212
Mount Shasta, CA 96067
800-299-9904
http://www.snowcrest.net/tognar/index.html
The funny and informative mail-order catalogue offers "the largest selection of ski and snowboard tuning/repair tools in the whole snowy world," plus waxes, how-to books and videos, clever tuning tips, and more. Direct merchant prices and knowledgeable, enthusiastic staff. If you plan to repair and maintain your board yourself, this is the first place to look for tuning equipment.

U.S. Geological Survey
P.O. Box 25286
Federal Center
Denver, CO 80225
800-872-6277
For current backcountry topographic maps.

Video Action Sports, Inc.
200 Suburban Road, Suite E
San Luis Obispo, CA 93401
800-727-6689
Video catalogue available.

WEB SITES

Not surprisingly, snowboarding has a strong presence on the World Wide Web. Keep in mind that on the Web, sites come and go — often they are as ephemeral as deep, untracked powder — and that sometimes information is dated or just plain wrong. Hopefully these sites will be around long enough to help jump-start your on-line snow-surfing safari.

Another tip: Try searching snowboard (or snowboarding) links; this will provide you with indexed hotlinks to new and exciting snowboard-related sites.

Transworld Snowboarding
http://twsnow.com
An e-zine by Transworld covering the entire sport, soup to nuts.

Snowboarding Online
http://www.solsnowboarding.com
Equipment reviews, industry news, rider profiles, classifieds, chat, and message boards.

http://www.rec.skiing.snowboard
FAQs, classifieds, news, and product reviews.

iSki-Inter Zine
http://www.iski.com
On-line ski magazine offering information on products and areas, and chat.

Skiing Source
http://paw.com.skiing
Winter resort information as well as the latest forecasts.

Ski Web
http://skiweb.com
Conditions, lodging, events, and reviews.

The Mountain Zone
http://www.mountainzone.com
Mountain sports, people, and activities.

Ski Industries America (SIA)
http://www.snowlink.com
Snowboard and ski product information.

National Ski Areas Association (NSAA)
http://www.travelbase.com.skiareas
Ski area and winter resort information.

Other Web sites
http://www.seismo.unr.edu/htdocs/weather.html
Highway conditions and weather forecasts.

http://cirrus.sprl.umich.edu.wxnet/radsat.html
Interactive weather maps from around the United States.

http://earthwatch.com/index.html
Topographic maps.

http://wxweb.msu.edu/weather
Current weather maps and movies.

AtPlay Snow Network
http://www.atplay.com
Snowboarding and skiing directory.

MAGAZINES

Snowboard Life
353 Airport Road
Oceanside, CA 92054
619-722-7777
A magazine written for a slightly older audience, *Snowboard Life* focuses on freeriding — with equal doses of carving, big-mountain riding, and air. Technique tips, equipment reviews, and adventure travel.

Snowboarder

33046 Calle Aviador
San Juan Capistrano, CA 92675
714-496-5922
Written for a young adult audience, *Snowboarder* covers all aspects of snowboarding and includes rider profiles, equipment reviews, adventure travel, technique tips, resort coverage, and competition. Freestyle, air, and big-mountain riding are the focus.

Transworld Snowboarding

353 Airport Road
Oceanside, CA 92054
619-722-7777
A magazine that chronicles all aspects of snowboarding. Adventure, rider profiles, equipment, technique tips, resort information, competition results, and great photography. Freestyle, air, and big-mountain riding are the focus. Primarily targets young adults, although it is a useful resource for anyone interested in the sport.

Snowboard Canada

2255 B Queen Street E, Suite 3266
Toronto, Ontario
Canada M4E 1G3
416-698-0138
Equipment and resort reviews, personalities, adventure, technique tips, and competition results. Written for a slightly older audience than many domestic snowboard publications, with a unique, north-of-the- border flavor — eh?

Transworld Snowboarding Business

353 Airport Road
Oceanside, CA 92054
619-722-7777
Addresses the business side of the sport. Industry news, people, retail tips, market studies, and tuning tips.

Ski Tech

P.O. Box 1125
Waitsfield, VT 05673
802-496-7700
Presents useful tips on equipment repair, tuning, and maintenance for shop technicians, retailers, and anyone interested in getting top performance from their equipment.

Backcountry

7065 Dover Way
Arvada, CO 80004
303-424-5858
A great magazine covering backcountry skiing and snowboarding. Adventure travel, safety tips, equipment reviews, destinations, and writing that captures the exciting yet serene essence of backcountry riding.

Couloir

P.O. Box 2349
Truckee, CA 96160
916-582-1884
http://www.couloir-mag.com
(check out the links section)
This magazine covers the backcountry beat, featuring extreme and exotic adventuring from around the world. Destinations, equipment reviews, backcountry safety, and adventure travel conspire to make you want to get out there yourself.

Powder

P.O. Box 1028
Dana Point, CA 92629
Always great photos, humor, and occasional snowboarding coverage, *Powder* tries to present an insider's view of the snow sport scene.

INSTRUCTIONAL VIDEOS

For those times when you're not actually out there riding, you'll find no shortage of snowboarding videos featuring huge cliff drops, insane chutes, and radical freestyle maneuvers (all scored to the latest headbanging tunes). While you can learn a lot from watching these videos, the following instructional videos specifically target the needs of learners. Because technique (and instruction) has evolved along with equipment, it's a good idea to view the most current videos for the best information.

How to Snowboard

Transworld, 1996. An informative instructional video for beginners. As of this writing, Transworld is assembling a sequel (as yet untitled) detailing advanced-level riding. Call 619-722-7777 for more info. and to order.

Boarding School

ETC Films, Brackendale, British Columbia, Canada, 1994. An informative, fun, and oft-times irreverent snowboard instruction video for beginners.

Snowboarding Images

AASI Videos, 303-987-9390. This video is used by the American Association of Snowboard Instructors to train snowboard teaching professionals. It clearly shows the application of key movements from beginner to advanced levels. This is an instructional video without words — just music and riding.

MANUFACTURERS

As of this writing, there are over three hundred entities manufacturing or selling snowboards. While some of the more recent entries into the field produce good products, these particular manufacturers have been around for a while. They have a history of producing quality products — and standing behind them.

Airwalk

1540A East Pleasant Valley Boulevard
Altoona, PA 16602
814-943-6164
http://www.airwalk.com

Barfoot Snowboards

5156 N. Commerce Avenue
Moorpark, CA 93021
888-222-7366
http://www.barfoot.com

Blax Step-In Snowboard Bindings/Generics Snowboards

30 A 6th Road
Woburn, MA 01801
617-937-9979

Burton Snowboards

80 Industrial Parkway
Burlington, VT 05401
800-881-3138
http://www.burton.com

Device Step-In Snowboard Bindings

8160 304th Avenue, SE
Preston, WA 98050
206-222-6351
http://www.ridesnowboards.com

K2 Snowboards

19215 Vashon Highway SW
Vashon, WA 98070
206-463-3631
http://www.k2sports.com

Lib Tech/Gnu Snowboards

2600 West Commodore
Seattle, WA 98199
206-270-9792
http://www.mervin.com

Morrow Snowboards

P.O. Box 12606
Salem, OR 97309
503-375-9300
http://www.mrrw.com

Nale Snowboards

P.O. Box 4279
208 Flynn Avenue
Burlington, VT 05401
802-863-5593

Nitro Snowboards

408 Columbia Street
Hood River, OR 97031
541-386-4006
http://www.nitrousa.com

Original Sin Snowboards

Box 25
Hercules Drive
Colchester, VT 05446
802-655-2400
http://www.originalsin.com

Oxygen Snowboards

9 Columbia Drive
Amherst, NH 03031
800-258-5020
http://www.pureoxygen.com

Ride

8160 304th Avenue, SE
Preston, WA 98050
206-222-6351
http://www.ridesnowboards.com

Rossignol Snowboards

P.O. Box 298
Industrial Avenue
Williston, VT 05495
802-863-2511
http://www.rossignol
snowboards. com

Salomon North America, Inc.

400 E. Main Street
Georgetown, MA 01833
800-225-6850
http://www.salomonsports.com

Sims Snowboards

22105 23rd Drive SE
Mill Creek, WA 98021
206-951-2700
http://www.simsnow.com

Switch Step-In Snowboard Bindings

P.O. Box 77006
San Francisco, CA 94107
415-777-9415
http://www.switch-sf.com

photocredits

Brian Bailey: 142
John Bing: 75, 76, 80, 109, 115, 117, 128
Courtesy of Burton Snowboards: 14, 23 (bottom), 24 (both), 25 (both), 26 (top), 27, 30 (both), 31
Courtesy of BXI: 15 (left)
Courtesy of Device: 26 (bottom)
Barrie Fisher: 12 (both)
John Goodman: 7, 11 (all), 19 (all), 21 (right), 23 (top, center), 32, 39 (all), 40 (both), 41 (both)

John Goodman/courtesy of Climb High: 34, 139
Paul Graves archival: 9 (both)
John Kelly: 72, 77, 78, 95, 111
Brian Litz: 136, 138, 144
Sherm Poppen: 10
Scott Spiker: 2, 4, 8, 35, 79, 81, 82, 83, 85, 124, 135, 143
Becky Luigart-Stayner: 137
Richard Walch: 98

Gordon Wiltsie: 13, 15 (right), 17, 18, 21 (left), 36, 37, 45 (all), 46, 47, 49, 50 (all), 51 (all), 54, 55, 56, 58 (all), 60, 62 (all), 63 (all), 65, 66, 68 (all), 69 (all), 87, 88, 89 (all), 91 (all), 92, 93 (all), 96, 97 (all), 99 (all), 103, 104, 105, 106 (both), 108, 110, 112 (all), 113 (bottom), 116 (all), 121 (all), 123, 126, 127 (all), 129, 131, 132, 141, 147, 148, 149, 151, 153 (both)

acknowledgments

Many people help to make a book. This particular one could not have happened without the talent, effort, and patience of John Barstow, my editor. To him I offer my grateful appreciation.

Thanks also to the members and staff of the American Association of Snowboard Instructors (AASI) and the Professional Ski Instructors of America (PSIA), whose passion and enthusiasm for snow sliding sports have been sources of both elucidation and inspiration.

Thanks to the following, who helped to make this book a reality: Bud and Lucie LaPorte Keene, Ted Fleischer, Cindy Hirschfeld, Sherm Poppen, Paul Graves, Barry Dugan, Natalie Gerstein, Jake Carpenter, and the staff at Burton Snowboards, B-Side, Nale Snowboards, and Rossignol Snowboards. Thanks also to Laurie Robinson, Kelly Hopkins, Brian Clark, Daniel Margaride, Rob and Jesse Mitchell, Vicki Benson, Jesse Seavers, Matthew Kopp, Josh Hooper, Denny Mabee, Ryan Radcliffe, Marco Olm, and Dan Wright. May your days be filled with sunshine, high peaks, and fresh powder!